SCIENCE SAFA NEW YORK CITY
Informal Science Expeditions for Children, Parents and Teachers

Ellie Miele, Ph.D
Jennifer D. Adams, Ph.D
Brooklyn College

Kendall Hunt
publishing company

Contents

Acknowledgements

AMNH for allowing images of the museum for use on the cover.
Prospect Park Alliance for allowing use of the map of Prospect Park the cover.
Jean Miele http://www.jeanmiele.com/ for cover photography and graphic design.

Planning for Science Learning in the Field

How to Use This Book

This book is intended as both a guide to teachers, parents, and guardians and as a field journal that children can use to record, organize, and reflect on their learning in informal environments. Students of education may want to practice using the trip sheets on their own excursions to parks and museums to see how these graphic organizers can help focus their own learning. The sheets have been created for general use and are not focused to particular exhibits at museums, parks, or zoos. Use the trip sheets as guides to creating your own trip sheets when planning units of instruction. You may want to be more specific, guiding students to particular exhibits that complement your lesson plans and learning objectives.

When planning trips, parents and teachers alike should review the science topics for the year and identify the science concepts you would like to reinforce with field experiences. Check the table in the back of this book for sites to consider for each science topic in the curriculum.

There are many parks with similar features. Your children may be most surprised and interested to learn about the nature closest to them. You can find forested areas, lakes and ponds, and wetland marshes in each of the five boroughs. Even Manhattan still boasts a small salt marsh in Inwood Hill Park. It may also interest children to see how similar the ecosystems are in each of the five boroughs. This can help reinforce an understanding that the entire city is within one climate zone.

Use the overviews of city parks, beaches, salt marshes, and zoos to get ideas for how to use zoos, parks, and museums to teach key science concepts in the elementary science curriculum. Use the planning ideas to help you organize your trips. Review the safety guidelines as you plan.

Use the trip sheets provided for children to complete to help them engage, explore, extend, and evaluate their learning experiences at museums, parks, and other living museums. Feel free to use these trip sheets as guides to create your own trip sheets for special needs.

You may want to plan trips to both parks and museums as part of a single unit of study. You can also use a series of trips to a single site to study the changing seasons.

Cultural and Natural Resources for Science Learning

New York City is probably the museum capital of the world. The city is also home to many of the world's most beautiful urban parks—with woodlands, meadows, marshes, lakes, and ponds—thanks to the forethought of the city's planners. It is also home to the National Parks of New York Harbor, with nearly 27,000 acres of natural coastal habitat. This wealth of resources provides recreation and entertainment, but it also supports science learning.

How do these cultural and natural resources help us to teach children science?

Science educators agree that the elementary science learning is best accomplished through a hands-on and minds-on approach to learning. Students learn most effectively when they are actively engaged in the discovery process. Experiences should provide students with opportunities to interact with the natural world to help them construct explanations about their world. This allows children to develop positive science attitudes and skills and to learn new science content in a way that capitalizes on their natural curiosity.

The traditional focus on memorization of special scientific terminology is less important than the development of an understanding of important concepts and relationships, and the ability to apply science skills and concepts in new contexts. Future formal state assessments are expected to test students' ability to explain, analyze, and interpret scientific processes and phenomena more than their ability to recall specific facts.

In practice, this means that parents and teachers can help children develop essential knowledge and skills through many different paths. For example, if one goal of the science curriculum is to help children learn to observe, organize, and analyze the components of an ecosystem, we may reach this goal by examining, comparing, and contrasting local temperate forests and coastal wetlands as fruit-fully as reading about tropical rainforests. The relationship between organisms and the non-living components of their environment is the unifying concept. Key under-standings such as interdependence of living organisms in ecosystems can be developed by examining any ecosystem. We hope to see a transfer of skills from one related context to the next. Does the child demonstrate an understanding that plants will be the primary producers in both meadows and forests?

Museums allow children access to artifacts, recreations, and multimedia representation of objects and organisms from around the world. Exhibits at museums and zoos offer children the opportunity to observe, compare, and contrast ecosystems from around the world in a single visit.

Children who have observed the bedrock outcrops of Manhattan schist or Inwood marble can compare the local rock to collections from around the world at the Rose Center for Earth and Space of the American Museum of Natural History. When visiting the Metropolitan Museum of Art or the Brooklyn Museum, they may compare the stone used in art and artifacts from around the world to our local rocks. They may even notice local rocks used in the construction of retaining walls and foundations in Lower Manhattan. When traveling, they may collect local rocks. Traveling in Maine, children may notice that the local rocks and mountains look like many of the rocks found on our rocky beaches. Can you help them imagine these rocks travelling to New York City on a river of ice when wooly mammoths roamed the Earth?

Good science instruction, whether formal or informal, should foster the development of science process skills and attitudes. The application of these skills empowers students to investigate important issues in the world around them. Essential components of the scientific attitude are objectivity, logic, and the use of evidence. No matter how wonderful nature may be, it is not magical. Encourage children to use observation and logic to make inferences (tentative conclusions based on knowledge and reason) about their findings.

Explore with your children. Help your children to observe, using sight, sound, and touch to identify properties of an object. Help them to compare, contrast, organize, and classify objects and organisms. Help them to count and measure. Help them to collect and interpret data, looking for patterns and relationships. Help them to speak, write, and draw like young naturalists. Help them to use what they have learned to make predictions about new experiences and places they plan to visit.

Have fun on your science expeditions exploring the great cultural and natural resources of the City of New York.

Theories of Learning in Informal Contexts

Think about your most memorable experiences with science. What comes to mind? Do you remember a TV show that piqued your interest about whales? Or was it a trip to the beach where you discovered the different colors in grains of sands? Perhaps it was a visit to a museum where you saw giant dinosaur fossils. Most of us will recall learning or interacting with science in an informal setting.

In *Learning Science in Informal Environments: People, Places, and Pursuits* (National Academies Press, 2009), the authors assert that the majority of science learning takes place in out-of-school settings, including in designed spaces such as museums, zoos, or science centers. These are places that allow us to pursue our interests in science in personally meaningful ways. In addition, we also learn science while doing everyday activities, such as gardening and painting, even though the goal of the activity is not necessarily to learn science. Informal environments are powerful tools for increasing interest in science. Think about how much more interesting it is to learn about trees in a park than to look at pictures and read a book. It is not that the latter is not an important learning activity, but think about how much more motivated children would be to read books about trees if they also had opportunities to study trees in a park using tools and methods similar to those that scientists use to study trees.

John Falk, a leading researcher in learning in informal environments, describes these experiences as *free-choice*—self-paced learning that allows the learner to pursue his/her own interests and inquiries. Learning in informal environments is a lifelong process that allows learners to participate in their own education in ways quite different than in a traditional classroom. One of the early theories about learning in informal environments, the Contextual Model of Learning, describes four interacting contexts that characterize learning in informal environments: (1) the personal, (2) the sociocultural, (3) the physical, and (4) the temporal.

Personal

Think about your last trip to a museum or a natural environment. You may remember times when you visited the same or similar places with your family as a child or on class trips. Perhaps an object, such as a meteorite, may prompt you to recall a movie your saw about space exploration. We bring our personal experiences to bear when learning in informal environments. All of our experiences make our learning experiences unique, and the shared nature of learning in an informal environment allows our personal experiences to become a part of the collective learning. More recently, the informal science education field has been recognizing the importance of identity in informal science learning. Not only do informal science environments allow us to express our identities (by allowing us to choose the objects/experiences that we wish to pursue), but informal environments also have the potential for affording young people opportunities to build positive identities around science. This is because young people often have successful interactions with science (fun, engaging, meaningful) in informal learning environments.

Sociocultural

The next time you visit an informal science institution or environment, note how children are interacting with one another in ways that are very different from the ways they interact in the classroom. They run from exhibit to exhibit. They show one another things that they have discovered while playing with the exhibit. They talk to one another and they learn from one another. Learning is a highly social and culturally embedded activity. We learn in our interactions with one another and we learn about things our culture deems valuable. Informal environments are such that they allow these important sociocultural interactions to happen naturally, much like what happens on a playground.

Physical

The places that we call informal science learning environments are designed places, like museums and science centers. These places were created with specific education goals in mind, usually to increase the public understanding of science. Institutions like zoos, aquaria, and botanical gardens—sometimes called living museums—may also have additional goals of increasing public awareness of conservation and biodiversity issues. Natural areas, such as parks and beaches, can also be considered informal learning environments because they are places where people learn about how the natural world works. Whether designed or natural, all of these places described have specific physical characteristics that make them spaces of novel learning interactions.

Temporal

Simply put, this is our learning across a lifespan. Every time we engage in a learning activity, we bring our personal and collective history of what we know and we use our learning of that activity to imagine our futures.

Although we described these as four distinct contexts, these contexts overlap in any informal science learning experience. For example, when we take our students to the beach to learn about erosion, we—ourselves and our students—bring our memories of going to beaches and what we already know about how erosion works, including any individual encounters we have had with erosion (personal). We interact with others collecting evidence of erosion; in these interactions, we tell our stories and share what we know and are learning about erosion (sociocultural). We are in a natural physical space that has evidence of erosion, which allows us to use our senses to learn about how the natural world works (physical). Finally, this experience is merely one moment in our continuum of learning about beaches, erosion, and the workings of the natural world (temporal).

Informal science environments have the potential of increasing science interest and participation in our nation. For this reason, several national reports call for greater integration of informal science environments with K-12 classrooms. In other words—get your students out of the classroom to learn and explore science!

Planning Trips for School Groups

Integrate

School trips to informal sites have traditionally been viewed as end-of-year rewards and not as instructional time. This narrow view is changing as classroom teachers and school administrators increasingly heed the call of science education experts to integrate place-based learning in the science curriculum. The value of learning with the real thing makes museums and parks natural extensions of the classroom. Museums have access to artifacts such as fossils, meteors, rocks, and minerals that schools cannot provide. Incorporate visits to informal sites into your teaching plan. Pre- and post-visit activities ensure a seamless transition between the informal learning experiences and the classroom. For example, during a unit on animal adaptations, students could plan a trip to a museum, zoo, or park to observe how animals are adapted to live in different environments. The pre-visit lessons could include a whole-class discussion about animal characteristics and adaptations. Frame the trip like a scientific expedition to observe animals in their natural habitats. Follow-up activities could include additional student reading and research, presentations about their learning, discussions of observations, and questions for further inquiry. Encourage students to continue their inquiry by visiting different sites with their families.

Practice

Students should have opportunities to practice inquiry, observing, and recording skills before their trip into the field. Although very valuable for student learning, field trips can be very distracting because of the novelty of the experience. Therefore, it would be beneficial to have students first practice in the classroom the skills that you would like them to use in the field. A useful exercise would be to have students look at a picture of a scene from a nature magazine or watch a clip from a nature video. You can ask them questions such as, "What do you see?" or "How do you know what season it is?" or "What do you think is going to happen next?" to get them thinking and discussing beyond— the practice of making inferences. You can bring in objects such as acorns, leaves, shells, etc.—objects that you or your students collect—and ask them to draw, label, categorize, and ask questions about what they observe. Take them on a mini expedition around the school. Inside the building, they can use their observations to learn as much about the cafeteria or library as possible, or they could go outside and observe the living things around the school building. These are a few exercises that can get students in the habit of observing, recording, and asking questions—skills that will make a field trip a more valuable learning experience. You may also want to practice following class rules for field trips on short expeditions in or around the school. Minor reminders and adjustments can be made in a lower-stakes context. If your students are ready to be serious and have practiced and know your expectations, your first trip is more likely to be a successful and positive experience for you and your students.

Go Online

Many informal science institutions and natural sites have websites that provide up-to-date information for visitors. The institution websites provide information about current and upcoming exhibits, floor plans, curriculum resources, and activities. Many parks have websites that provide maps, background information, and a schedule of upcoming events and educational programs. These prove useful resources for field trips and general curriculum planning.

Visit

If possible, visit your field trip site ahead of time. This can be a fun activity with friends or family during holidays. Review the different exhibits or places that you would like to use with your students. Decide how and where you will assemble your students to facilitate their learning experience, keeping in mind that many sites mentioned in the book—especially the zoos and museums—tend to be crowded with other school groups. If you want your students to work in groups, have them form working groups before the field trip. Try to find locations where small groups can work at different exhibits while you can keep an eye on all of them. Remember, it may be difficult to find quiet corners in museums and zoos for last-minute instructions.

Less Is More

Rather than trying to see the whole site in one visit, pick a selected number of exhibits, a hall, or a specific place that meets your particular learning goals. Encourage your students to really document what they observe. You may want to provide them with a few tools to help their observations, such as flashlights, rulers, and colored pencils in addition to site-specific tools.

Frame Guiding Questions

Guiding questions are a great way to focus a field trip. The field trip could be framed as an expedition with students going on a search for clues or answers to inquiries that they may have generated during pre-trip activities. Guiding questions also model how scientific research often starts with observations, then leads to questions and a search for answers that often lead to more questions.

Free Time!

Because a field trip may be novel for students (even if they've been to the site before, there is always something "old" to see again or new to discover), it is important to allow students to freely explore some places of personal interest to encourage the sense of curiosity and wonder about the natural world. You can also integrate some free choice within your learning objectives. For instance, if your class is studying rocks in the Hall of Planet Earth at the American Museum of Natural History, you could have each student pick a favorite rock. They can become the expert about this rock and report to the class at sharing time on what they learned. Scope out the exhibits you plan to visit and think about how you can include choice for your students. This can promote a spirit of lifelong learning and the sense of science learning for personal enjoyment.

Some other practical considerations for informal science institution field trips:

General considerations

- Get parent permissions—Each school has procedures for doing this. Some have a uniform permission form, while others require you to make your own permission form.

- Get administrative permission and clearances—Check with your administration about which procedures are required to book a trip. Are only a certain number of classes allowed out per day? Are you required to hire a school bus?

- Plan and reserve transportation—Are you going to walk? Use public transportation? Reserve a school bus? Whatever mode of transportation you plan to use, get the necessary passes and/or make the necessary reservations. Carefully plan the route that you will take and make sure that the school, parents, and chaperones are aware of your route.

- Consider using travel time as instructional time—Will you pass interesting landmarks along your route? Have a trip sheet to keep students occupied during travel.

Logistics: Plan and prepare!

- Reserve a date and/or program at the institution—Due to safety reasons, many institutions limit the number of classes that can visit on any given day. It is important that you reserve as early as possible. You should also check to see if the halls and exhibits you wish to visit are open, as they are sometimes closed for renovations or special events.

- Food—A field trip with a bunch of hungry students is not a pleasant experience. Be sure to make arrangements for lunch. Some institutions require that you reserve a space for lunch, whether you are bringing lunch or purchasing it on site. If you plan on telling students to bring lunch money, keep in mind that cafeterias at the cultural institutions tend to be pricey as this is an important source of revenue. Check in advance the lunch options in and near the institution. If you are in a public school, you also have the option of bringing the school lunch. Check with your administrator for the procedures for doing this.

- Reserve chaperones—Some institutions have a required student/adult ratio.

- Identification tags—Make sure that each student is wearing an identification tag with the information your school requires—at least the name, address, and phone number of your school.

For outdoor explorations

- Make sure that you are adequately prepared and that your students dress according to the weather and the activities planned. Generally, everyone should wear sturdy, close-toed shoes, a hat, and a jacket.

- Water, sunscreen, and insect repellant are all important items to have on a field exploration. You might need to carry extra for students who forget or run out.

- Have an alternative plan in case of inclement weather.

- Be aware of safety hazards that you may encounter on the trip and brief students ahead of time about proper behavior in the field.

- Carry a first aid kit and emergency contact information for all students.

Planning Trips for Families

Visiting the city's museums, zoos, botanical gardens, and natural green spaces is a wonderful way to spend quality family time. Not only does it provide the opportunity to play together, but it also provides a valuable time for family science learning! Believe it or not, much of the science that we know is learned in informal settings throughout our lifetime. Pursuing hobbies, family activities, and watching nature shows on TV are just some of the ways we engage in science learning in our daily lives. Taking your child on field trips to museums, zoos, and parks can support you child's schoolwork and help your child succeed. Parents of children with special needs can build on school learning by selecting "free-choice" expeditions that reinforce concepts studied in class.

Children are naturally curious and visiting science-rich places and spaces with them is a great way to foster this sense of wonder about the natural world. Use this book to help select excursions that will let your child apply his school learning outside of school. Let your child teach you what she has learned in school on field trips. If your child is studying temperate forests, go to a local park that has natural wooded areas. Compare wooded areas at the shore to inland parks. Go to the American Museum of Natural History and visit the North American Forests exhibit to observe life-like reproductions of forest life below the ground and in all seasons.

If your child is studying the water cycle, take her to see real lakes, ponds, and rivers. If your child is studying oceans, imagine the excitement in his eyes when he sees the large model of the blue whale at the American Museum of Natural History. These informal science-learning experiences could spark a lifetime of interest in science.

Families living in or near New York City have access to a wealth of science-rich informal learning opportunities. Although careful planning allows you to maximize your trip, a spontaneous excursion can also bring delightful surprises. What follows are some general tips for planning family visits to informal science places and taking advantage of the free-choice learning environment that these places offer:

- Know what you child is studying in school. Communicate with your child's teacher about what she is learning in science. Review your child's science notes and textbooks.

- Plan your explorations to complement what your child is doing in school.

- Use this book to select some possible sites to visit.

- Visit the websites of the places you plan to visit. Many of them offer fun and engaging free or low-cost programming for families. In addition, websites often offer online interactives or activities that complement the site-based exhibits and allow you to begin and/or continue your explorations at home.

- Plan your visit for early in the day, especially in the summer months, as popular places tend to get crowded.

- Bring a digital camera and journal (or this book) to help document your trip. Perhaps start a photo album, scrapbook, or slide show to document your family's science adventures!

- Listen to your child; allow her to guide explorations. Children are often the facilitators of family learning in informal settings.

- Encourage your child to further his investigations by asking leading questions:
    o What do you notice about…?
    o What would happen if…?
    o Why do you think…?
    o What do you already know about…?
    o What else would you like to know about…?
    o How do you think we could find out…?

- Participate in the learning experience with your child—you might just learn something new! Don't be afraid to push buttons, turn knobs, or read the text to find out more information about what you observe. This is a great way to model the joy of being a life-long learner for your child.

- Take advantage of your local library and Internet resources to continue your explorations when you return home. This might encourage a repeat visit to your science-learning site!

- Plan what you will do to eat. Hungry children are often unfocused and fussy children. Keep in mind that cafeterias in many institutions tend to be expensive and have limited selections. You may want to bring your own snacks or lunch.

- Always remember to keep it fun! One of the novelties of learning in informal spaces is the free-choice nature—it is self-guided and based on the interests of the visitor. Allow your child to pursue her own interests and be prepared for an interesting journey!

Science Safety in the Field

These are basic guidelines for safe practices in doing science investigations in field settings. Always plan ahead. Always model the behaviors you expect from your child or students.

Safety with Plants

When working in the field with plants, never touch plants that are unfamiliar. Always wash hands after working with seeds and plants. Never put seeds or plants in the mouth. Do not handle seeds or plants without hand protection if there are cuts or sores on the hands.

Be particularly alert to plant safety on field trips. Be aware of plants in the local area that are harmful. Learn how to identify poison ivy, a very common poisonous local plant. Be aware of the signs of plant poisoning and act quickly if a child exhibits such signs after a field trip. Symptoms may include one or more of the following: headache, nausea, dizziness, vomiting, skin eruption, itching, or other skin irritation.

Many local plants generate pollens that can cause sneezing, itchy, watery eyes, or can worsen asthma symptoms. Some people may also get skin rashes from direct contact with pollens or leaves of certain plants. Usually mild allergic symptoms may be worsened by direct contact. Allergic individuals should shower and change and wash clothing after outdoor investigations to remove pollen from skin, hair, and clothing. Adults should plan ahead for possible allergic symptoms in consultation with the family physician. It may be prudent to take an antihistamine before leaving home for a field investigation. Teachers cannot take responsibility for students' medication and cannot allow students to self-medicate.

Safety with Animals

All handling of animals by children should be done voluntarily and only under immediate adult supervision. A lesson on proper care and treatment of the animal should be given to children before they study animals in the wild. Always model and require humane treatment of animals.

In general, animals caught in the wild should not be brought into the home or classroom. For example, turtles are carriers of salmonella, and many wild mammals are subject to rabies. Wild birds are protected by law and must not be caged. If you see a sick or injured animal or bird, you should contact a certified wildlife rehabilitator or the Audubon Society. You may collect invertebrates that are known to be harmless, such as earthworms or pillbugs, for brief observation, but they should be returned to the exact place where they were collected.

On field trips or during other outdoor activities, be aware of the potential hazards of insect bites, such as allergic reactions to bee stings. Teachers should always inform parents in advance of any upcoming field trips and ask about students' histories of allergies to insects. Be aware, too, of diseases spread by fleas or ticks. Dress appropriately to limit tick access to legs. Do not allow children to touch ants, spiders, or caterpillars.

Emergency Procedures

Make plans in advance to handle possible emergencies when you are in the field. Be sure that equipment and supplies needed for foreseen emergencies are on hand.

At minimum, classroom teachers should establish emergency first-aid procedures for cuts and scrapes, poisoning, and bites. All classroom teachers should know how to notify appropriate authorities and response agencies in the event of an emergency.

Safety Rules

Children usually follow rules that have been collaboratively developed more willingly than rules that appear arbitrary. One way to "decide" on rules for safe science trips is to encourage children to first brainstorm, and then discuss why rules are necessary and what kind of dangers there might be in doing science in the field. If an important rule is not identified by children during this process, the adult can ask leading questions such as, "What might happen if you did not know where your adult companion was?" Children must realize that safety rules for school or family trips are important to protect their own safety as well as their classmates and others. Students who do not follow the rules may lose the privilege of taking part in field trips and may even limit their class's opportunities to learn outside the classroom. Children and parents should sign a Field Trip Safety Contract. Always review your safety rules again before embarking on any field trip.

Suggested Safety Rules for Science Field Trips

1. Wear appropriate clothing for field activities, including long pants, sturdy shoes, and socks. Bring additional clothing in case of cool or wet weather.
2. Use sunscreen and insect repellent if appropriate.
3. Do not fool around during science field trips. Stay focused.
4. Stay with your group.
5. Always keep your teacher, parent, or other responsible adult in sight.
6. Know where to go for shelter in case of thunderstorms.
7. Never touch plants or animals, including insects, without the approval and direct supervision of a responsible adult.

continued

8. Never taste anything during a field activity.

9. Never approach rivers, lakes, or ponds without the approval and direct supervision of a responsible adult.

10. Respect walls and fences—they are there to protect you or to protect the environment, not to sit or climb on.

11. Tell a responsible adult immediately if an accident occurs.

12. Clean up around you when your activity is finished. Leave nothing behind. Do not remove any plants or animals from the field. Return any creatures you observe to the same place you found them.

13. Wash your hands with soap and water as soon as possible after completing your field investigations.

14. Shower and check for ticks upon returning home from field investigations.

The Learning Cycle: Sequential Learning in Informal Settings

The Learning Cycle is a model of instruction that encourages children to move sequentially through learning experiences beginning with engagement and progressively increasing the depth and complexity of their thinking. The activities suggested throughout this book will use the Learning Cycle to help children gain deeper understandings of core science concepts through their informal field explorations. Activities will be organized to move sequentially through the cycles, always beginning with engagement and recall and moving to higher order thinking.

Three-phase Learning Cycle

- In Phase 1, *Exploration*, children are free to manipulate materials and explore scientific phenomena. Instruction on concepts is *not* given first. The adult facilitator poses open-ended questions to focus the child on key ideas. Children have the opportunity to develop their own hypotheses and to test them through observation.

- In Phase 2, *Concept Development*, children are guided to scientific understandings with guided activities, including comparing and contrasting and sorting and categorizing.

- In Phase 3, *Concept Application*, children apply the skills and knowledge gained during their initial discoveries to a related concept. This phase reinforces earlier learning.

A five-stage model, referred to as the "Five E's," includes a more explicit emphasis on both engagement and evaluation. These aspects of the Learning Cycle are especially important when exploring at museums and parks. Engagement may begin with the simple question "What would you like most to explore here today?" Evaluation may be reflective conversation on the way home, guided by questions such as "What was the most interesting thing you discovered today? Why is it important to you?"

- In Stage 1, *Engagement*, the cycle begins with identifying what children already know about the concepts to be explored. Children express their own understanding about a natural object, creature, or scientific concept.

- In Stage 2, *Exploration*, objects and phenomena are explored. Free exploration is followed by guided investigations.

- In Stage 3, *Explanation*, children explain their understanding of concepts and processes and demonstrate their current conceptual understanding.

- In Stage 4, *Elaboration*, children apply concepts in new and different contexts, and build on or extend understanding and skills. We will refer to this as *Expanding*.

- In Stage 5, *Evaluation*, children assess their understanding, skills, and abilities and formulate new questions.

The following pages provide simple trip sheets that you can use to help your children benefit from the Learning Cycle to deepen their learning on field trips to any location.

Using Key Questions

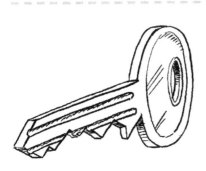

It has been said that play is the work of children, but making sense of the world is also the work of children, and they pursue this work diligently. This driving curiosity can become maddening, but it is a necessary first step to learning and should be nurtured, not discouraged. In order to develop the capacity for scientific reasoning in children, we must establish a conversation about the natural world and encourage the curiosity that we may have inadvertently discouraged. We must value the child's attempts to recognize the patterns of nature and welcome questions, even if we do not know the answers ourselves.

According to Russian psychologist Lev Vygotsky, a child learns the habits of mind of her/his culture through *social interactions* with significant people in her/his life. Vygotsky believed that there is a connection between speech and the development of mental concepts. Contemporary social psychologist Lauren Resnick suggests that reasoning skills may be developed through *accountable talk*, a form of discussion that occurs whenever speakers are expected to defend and justify their observations and conclusions through the use of evidence and logic.[1] We can use these ideas to nurture scientific thinking in children. To help children learn scientific habits of mind, we must engage them in conversations that follow the conventions of scientific discussions, with an emphasis on describing objective observations and using evidence and logic.

When talking about science with children, encourage them to describe specific observations that support their statements. For instance, on a walk around a lake, a child may say, "That bird looks like a duck." The child's comment tells you that the first step for learning has occurred. The child has *engaged* with the subject. This is an opportunity for a science talk. To keep the conversation going, you might answer, "What is it about that bird that reminds you of a duck?" The child may have observed a familiar duck-like shape or may have noticed a unique adaptation such as webbed feet or a duck-like bill adapted for grazing in water. The key question unlocks deeper learning. Depending on what the child has noticed, you might follow up with, "How might webbed feet help birds swim?" or "Why do you think water birds have flat beaks?" If the child is still engaged in observation and thinking about this bird, you can continue the conversation with a simple question such as, "Is there anything else about this bird that reminds you of a duck?" or "How is this bird different than a duck?" You can also share an observation and an inference of your own. The use of key questions can help children articulate their observations and their reasoning and keep our conversations *scientific*. Key questions will not ask children for simple yes or no or one-word responses, but will ask children to think more deeply about the subject and explore their own reasoning. A list of typical key questions is provided. Be sure to give the child time to think and talk, and take the time to listen to the response.

---

[1] Michaels, S., O'Connor, C. and Resnick, L. (2008). Deliberative Discourse Idealized and Realized: Accountable Talk in the Classroom and in Civic Life. *Studies in Philosophy and Education.* 27, 283-297.

What do you notice about this place, plant, animal or thing?

How would you describe this place, plant, animal or thing to a friend?

Can you think of more ways to describe it?

What color(s) or patterns does it have?

Does it have a special texture?

How would you describe its size?

Do you think this place, plant, animal or thing will change or stay the same?

What might make it change?

In what ways is this place, plant, animal or thing special?

What made you notice this place, plant, animal or thing?

What other things interact with this plant, animal or thing?

How do you think people interact with this plant, animal or thing?

Does this place, plant, animal or thing remind you of another one?

In what ways is it similar? In what ways is it different?

How does this animal behave?

Can this animal live in a wide range of habitats?

What do you think this animal eats?

What questions do you have about this place, plant, animal or thing?

How do you think you could find out more about this place, plant, animal or thing?

Engage

What I know about _____.

What I wonder about _____.

 **Explore**

NAME:

DATE:

LOCATION:

What I observed about _____.

Explain

Based on my observations, I think that...

Expand

Compare two objects or creatures and write down as many ways as you can that they are similar.

Now write down as many ways as you can that they are different.

 **Evaluate**

NAME:

DATE:

LOCATION:

The Most Interesting Things I learned...

What are the most interesting things you learned from your trip?
Why were they interesting to you?

Museums

The American Museum of Natural History

The mission of the American Museum of Natural History is to discover, interpret, and disseminate—through scientific research and education—knowledge about human cultures, the natural world, and the universe.

Since the founding of the American Museum of Natural History in 1869, education has always been central to its mission. From the late 1800s to the present, the Museum has offered specialized programs for schools and teachers. Recently, the Museum established the Gottesman Center for Teaching and Learning, which houses a host of programs for teachers, schools, students, and families ranging from after-school programs to professional development for educators. The National Center for Science Literacy Education and Technology (NCSLET) creates and maintains a catalogue of new media resources that brings the work of museum scientists to the public. These include Science Bulletins (interactive media about cutting-edge scientific research), Seminar on Science (distance learning science content courses), and Ology (an interactive science and anthropology website for children). Many of these resources are catalogued in Resources for Learning, an online catalogue of free educational resources produced by the Museum and which can be accessed via the Museum's website.

Many visitors associate the Museum with the numerous artifacts and exhibits that are on display in the halls. However, much of this would not be possible without the wealth of scientific research and data collection that happens behind-the-scenes. Over 200 scientific personnel, including over 40 tenure-track curators, are involved in research activities ranging from paleontological expeditions to the Gobi Desert to mapping the evolutionary relationships between living things on the "tree of life." The Museum maintains stewardship of over 32 million specimens and artifacts from around the globe, many of them dating back to the founding days of the Museum. The Museum is on the cutting edge of research and, as a result, is a good place to see how science changes as new discoveries are made. For example, Museum scientists contributed to the current understanding that the dinosaurs did not actually all become extinct—birds are their living descendents!

The Museum is a large complex covering four square city blocks. With numerous halls and exhibits focusing on the diversity of life on Earth, it is a great place for children to learn about animal characteristics and adaptations. The halls are organized either by scientific themes or geographic areas.

In the Hall of Planet Earth, children can explore the processes that shape our planet. They can touch the banded iron rock and view the layers of red jasper and the black layers of magnetite—ask children to explain what this tells them about the history of our planet. These rocks were formed as plants first began to evolve and fill the Earth's atmosphere with oxygen, and iron began to rust all over the planet. There are other tactile experiences in the hall, such as a relief globe of planet Earth where children can feel the Rocky Mountains and the Himalayas relative to sea level. Children can explore the hall and pick their favorite sedimentary, metamorphic, and igneous rocks. They can draw and describe them and explain what they have learned about the different ways that rocks form. In the Rose Center for Space, children can touch the Willamette meteorite. This giant iron mass traveled through space and streaked through the sky before landing on Earth. Explore the halls to find out how astronomers learn about objects in space.

The Halls of Ocean Life and Biodiversity are great places for children to learn about the diversity of life on the planet. The iconic blue whale hangs in the Hall of Ocean Life and is surrounded by eight dioramas of different aquatic ecosystems. Invite children to pick two of the dioramas and draw them. Then ask them

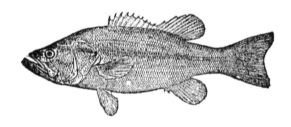

to describe how the physical environment is different in each. How is the diversity of life different? Why do they think one is more diverse than the other?

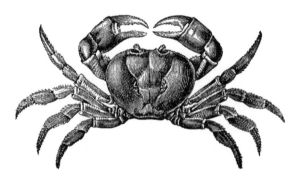

The Spectrum of Life wall in the Hall of Biodiversity shows the evolutionary relationship among living things. Here, children can pick two animals that they have never seen before and draw and describe them. Walk through the Rainforest Diorama to observe animal adaptations to a tropical rainforest. There are organisms at every level, from the canopy to the undergrowth. Like a

Science Safaris in New York City

real rainforest, it is dark—so bring a flashlight to help you investigate the diorama. Encourage children to listen to the sounds in the rainforest too—what do they hear?

Compare the Rainforest Diorama to one in the Hall of North American Forests or a local park. Make a list of the abiotic (i.e., temperature, average rainfall) and biotic (flora and fauna) factors found in each. Ask children why they think that the plants and animals are different in each biome? Learn about the relationships between large ants, grubs, millipedes, and their environment in the Life on the Forest Floor diorama in the Hall of North American Forests. The Hall of the New York State Environment is a classic hall that chronicles the development of the natural landscape over time. Observe changes in upstate New York over time. Ask children to think about what a diorama for today would look like. In the Spitzer Hall of Human Origins, children could explore how closely related we are to primates and how humans are unique.

Be sure to check out the mammal halls. The dioramas use preserved animal and plant specimens in the foreground merged with detailed background painting depicting an actual place and time. Children enjoy looking at these displays, from which they can learn much about animal characteristics and adaptations to global ecosystems. Have children compare the elephants and environments in the Hall of African Mammals to the ones in the Hall of Asian Mammals—how are they alike? How are they different? In the Hall of North American Mammals, children could compare the grizzly bear to the brown bear.

The Museum is also famous for its fossil halls. The fourth floor is designed so visitors can follow the path of evolution according to key evolutionary characteristics. Children can observe the fossils and learn about animal structure and form as well as ancient animal diversity and paleo-ecology. Fossils also tell us much about the plants and climate in which extinct mammals and reptiles lived. Paleontologists can infer much about the lives of extinct animals by comparing them to those alive today. How do paleontologists know that Tyrannosaurus rex was a flesh-eater? That Apatosaurus ate vegetation?

The cultural halls can be used to illustrate interactions between humans and the environment. For example, after visiting the Rainforest Diorama in the Hall of Biodiversity, you could visit the Mbuti Diorama in the Hall of African Peoples and/ or the Hall of South American Peoples to learn how people use materials in their environment to survive.

When planning your trip, be sure to visit the Museum's website (http://www.amnh.org/) as it has extensive resources about the Museum's visiting halls and behind-the-scenes research. You could begin with the Resources for Learning link, where resources are organized by content; you will find guides for educators for many of the halls and activities to extend your museum experience.

American Museum of Natural History visit planning notes:

New York Hall of Science

Located in Flushing Meadows Park, Corona Queens, The New York Hall of Science (NYSCI) was originally built as a pavilion for the 1964 World's Fair. This is New York City's only interactive science museum. It houses over 400 interactive exhibits that explore life science, chemistry, and physics; it is the largest collection of hands-on exhibits in New York City. When you visit the Hall, you will see young people wearing red aprons encouraging visitors to interact with the exhibits. These are Explainers, and they are a part of the Science Career Ladder, an innovative program that employs high school and college students to facilitate learning interactions with visitors at the Hall. Ask them a question!

Explore!

The NYSCI has a number of permanent exhibits that are organized into different themes. All of the exhibits are highly interactive and designed for touching, manipulating, and exploring, beckoning young scientists to learn and discover the world of science. In the Connections area, students explore the kinds of networks we encounter in our daily lives. There is a rope and pulley exhibit that demonstrates the role of forces in a network. Discover a City's Network and Powered by a Network are two exhibits that demonstrate networks, such as the electrical grid, train systems, and telephone networks that keep the city going. There are other exhibits that allow you to learn about the movement of the oceans, an active riverbed, and flocking behavior. This is an exciting area to explore how connections and networks influence our daily lives and our planet.

Feedback houses exhibits that explore mechanical engineering concepts and includes demonstrations of suspension bridges, propellers, and steam engines. Here you could learn about how a bridge, like the Brooklyn Bridge, uses suspension cables to support heavy vehicles and how a steam engine moves a train. You will also learn how steam engines played a key role in shaping the Industrial Revolution.

There are several themes that focus on things that are very important but that we cannot see with our naked eyes. Focusing on microbes, Hidden Kingdoms features Wentzscopes©, microscopes with large top lenses that allow several children to view living and moving microbes at once! Text panels and videos demonstrate the various roles of microbes in everyday life. In Marvelous Molecules, children can learn about how molecules carry out important life functions in all living things. The variety of molecules found in living things is vast, yet only 25 elements make up this diversity! With a short introductory video, hands-on demonstrations, and computer interactives, children can learn about how molecules allow for reproduction, movement, sensing, and creating energy to enable life functions in all living things. In the Realm of the Atom, children discover the atom—the building blocks of all matter—and learn about different physics concepts, such as Brownian motion, waves, and quantum physics. Using a spectroscope, children can compare different sources of light and learn about the role that atoms play in producing heat and light.

From here, it might be interesting to move on to Seeing the Light, a series of exhibits that allow children to learn about how the eye works—how humans are able to see light and color. This is a fun area where children can explore how light behaves, create and manipulate shadows, and learn how color is created. They can also learn about the structure and function of the human eye. An Explainer may even be there to demonstrate a cow's eye dissection. A cow's eye is similar to the human eye, but larger. This demonstration allows children to see the structure of the eye and learn about common malfunctions, such as cataracts and glaucoma.

Most of the exhibits allow children to get physical in learning science; however, this is most evident in the Sports Challenge exhibit and the Science Playground. In this exhibit area, children are encouraged to balance like a surfer, test a bouncing ball on different surfaces, and pitch a baseball, all while learning physics, physiology, and material science as applied to sports. Other exhibits challenge children to test their reaction time and compete in a computer simulated wheelchair race to learn about speed and test different wheelchair designs.

In the Rocket Park, children can see some of the iconic and historical rockets designed to explore space. These rockets were designed for the 1964–65 World's Fair and were cutting-edge space-exploring technology of the time. This is a nice complement to the Search for Life Beyond Earth exhibit, where children can learn about the search for life on other planets. Here they can explore the extreme environments that are found on Earth and the organisms that thrive there, as well as the possibilities that life could exist in similar environments found on other planets.

The New York Hall of Science is a wonderful place for children to become immersed in engaging science learning activities. It is a fun place with many different areas to explore. Encourage children to try things several times and note what happens. There are many things to manipulate at each exhibit. The Explainers do a good job of modeling learning interactions with exhibits—watch what they do! Plan to do some focused observations with children, but allow plenty of time for free-choice play and exploration.

Brooklyn Children's Museum

The Brooklyn Children's Museum, founded in 1899, was the first museum created expressly for children. It recently underwent a multimillion dollar renovation and expansion, and is the first LEED-Silver certified "green" museum in New York City. The museum serves and celebrates a diverse urban population as well as visitors and cultures from around the world from its off-the-beaten track location in Crown Heights, Brooklyn. The community is a high-density residential area with a predominantly Caribbean and Hasidic Jewish population.

The halls and exhibits throughout the museum are child-scaled, but designed to meet the needs of both school groups and families. Museum exhibits are based on best-practices in inquiry learning and provide many objects to touch and many simple and engaging activities. The mission of the museum encompasses both cultural and natural history and exhibits in both categories provide rich experiences in inquiry learning for toddlers and pre-schoolers through elementary grades. Middle schoolers will also have fun in the company of younger children. At the Brooklyn Children's Museum, children come first; little ones will not have to compete with teens and adults for access to exhibits.

The science exhibits focus on natural environments, animal form and function, water in the landscape, observation skills, and music and sound. Both cultural and natural exhibits offer opportunities to practice measurement skills with a variety of tools. The permanent collection of the museum includes nearly 30,000 cultural objects and natural-history specimens. The natural-history collection includes rocks, minerals, and fossils and skeletons, as well as mounted birds, mammals, and insects. Although many objects from the collection are behind glass, many are also at child-height displays and workstations, allowing children to both see and touch the specimens. Objects and animals are grouped to encourage children to compare and contrast similar specimens. Signs and spaces encourage young readers to draw their observations with paper and drawing materials provided. Adults can use these cues to guide children at exhibits. The artwork of visitors is on display throughout the museum.

A large stream table with a waterwheel and varied slopes flows through the main hallway, allowing whole-class observation of how water moves in the landscape. Children between 18 months and five years can explore water in Water Wonders, a water-play area with a large pond, and toys for pouring, measuring, and experimenting located in the Totally Tots area.

Many exhibits provide materials for role playing during or after direct observation of artifacts and living animals. Both realistic and stylized representations of plants and animals are featured. Children can hunt for seashells or plastic replicas of sea creatures in the saltmarsh beach area or compare fruits from around the world in the International Grocery store without worrying about bruising the bananas. Little ones who don't want to let go of role-playing materials at an exhibit can hold on to them until they leave the museum. A handy return box is located near the exit.

The Neighborhood Nature exhibit is an excellent place to explore the plants, animals, and landforms of the common local ecosystems in the New York City neighborhood. This exhibit provides a structured environment in which children can develop observation skills to apply in more complex environments such as the American Museum of Natural History, zoological parks, and the wild. Exhibits include an urban woodland, a freshwater pond, a saltwater beach, and a community garden. The Neighborhood Nature exhibit includes life-like dioramas, living animals, and role-playing areas. The urban woodland area invites children to build a bug with interchangeable plastic parts or to camouflage a paper insect and help it hide in different environments. Dioramas allow children to observe three-dimensional representations of natural ecosystems where the creatures will stay in sight for easy observation. Signs ask simple questions such as "How many plants and animals can you find?" Simple pictorial guides help young readers identify the birds, reptiles, mammals, and other creatures in the dioramas. For older children who want to know more, more detailed guides are available in the Science Inquiry Center.

The Pond Homes diorama allows children to observe a heron and aquatic turtles in a realistic pond environment reminiscent of those in the nearby Brooklyn Botanic Garden and Prospect Park. Children can crawl under the pond where they can watch live fish and turtles swim among aquatic plants. Special cameras and listening devices let children watch and listen for animals hidden throughout the diorama. Near the pond, a stream habitat with water flowing down a series of waterfalls shows how fish, muskrats, raccoons, and birds depend on water.

In the Saltwater Beach environment area, children can create marine animal models and test how they move in the wave pool. They can sift for clues to marine life in the sandy dunes area and then check nearby specimen samples to identify what they have found. Guided by museum educators, they can touch live horseshoe crabs and sea stars at the tide pool.

Role-playing activities in Neighborhood Nature include climbing inside a hollow log like a small burrowing mammal in the Urban Woodland exhibit, allowing a up-close look at underground organisms and live toads, snakes, and turtles that live under the forest floor. In the Community Garden, children dig, plant, and harvest play plants. Nearby, the Greenhouse and Outdoor Garden are filled with both common and exotic live plants, insects, and animals.

The museum offers a number of exhibits that allow children to explore sound and music. Children under five can make music with a variety of instruments in the Totally Tots area. They can also try talking with far-away friends on the walkie-talkie tube. School-age children can role-play being an environmental DJ by mixing the unique rhythms of human-made and natural outdoor sounds at the kid-friendly mixing board located in the Community Garden area. In the Global Beats Theater, children can compare and contrast musical instruments from around the world. They can join dancers in the life-size video projections of local dance troupes on a small performance stage, complete with a curtain and seating for a small audience. Children can select from a traditional Native American warrior dance, Russian ballet, Irish step dance, Arab *debkah*, Bangladeshi folk dances, and the local Gowanus Wildcats tap-dance troupe.

The museum website is written for use by children and offers the opportunity to view objects from the collection. Use the website to plan what to look for at the museum. The website also provides an embedded drawing application that children can use to draw many objects from the collection. Drawings may be sent electronically for publication on the museum website. http://www.brooklynkids.org/

Brooklyn Children's Museum visit planning notes:

Engage

What I want to see at the museum.

Why I want to see it.

 # Explore

NAME:

DATE:

LOCATION:

Comparing Objects

Many zoos, botanical gardens, and museums have exhibits with unusual objects. Choose two to observe, compare, and contrast.

Draw two objects below. How are they alike? How are they different?

Explore

Comparing Organisms

Many zoos, botanical gardens, and museums have exhibits with unusual plants or animals. Choose two to observe, compare, and contrast.

Draw two organisms below. How are they alike? How are they different?

Comparing Ecosystems

Many zoos, botanical gardens and museums have exhibits that recreate ecosystems. Choose two to observe, compare and contrast.

Draw one ecosystem below.

Describe the climate: amount of sunshine, rain, average temperature, seasonal change. If this is an aquatic environment, is it freshwater or saltwater, moving or still?

How have animals adapted to this environment?

Explore

NAME:

DATE:

LOCATION:

Comparing Ecosystems

Draw one ecosystem below.

Describe the climate: amount of sunshine, rain, average temperature, seasonal change. If this is an aquatic environment, is it fresh water or salt, moving or still?

How have animals adapted to this environment?

Comparing and Contrasting Ecosystems
How are these ecosystems the same?
How are these ecosystems different?

 # **Explore**

NAME:

DATE:

LOCATION:

Observing Rocks

You will find rocks at museums and parks. Select four rocks that you like. Try to use words to describe them so that someone would be able to pick your rock out of a collection. If your rock is from a museum, write down what kind it is. If it is from a park, try to find out what kind of rock it is from a field guide.

This rock is _____.	This rock is _____.
This rock is _____.	**This rock is _____.**

Expand

NAME:

DATE:

LOCATION:

Dichotomous Sorting of Objects or Organisms

Pick a property you observed that only some things have. Use it to sort the things you observed into two groups, those with that property and those without. Record your work with words and/or drawings in each column. Select another property and try again.

With Property _____.	Without Property _____.

Select another property and sort the objects above again in the two columns below.

With Property _____	Without Property _____	With Property _____	Without Property _____

Evaluate

NAME:

DATE:

LOCATION:

The Most Interesting Things I Learned

What are the most interesting things you learned from your trip to the museum?

Chapter 3

What You Can Learn at the Zoo

New York City has a zoological park in each of the five boroughs as well as an aquarium devoted to aquatic animals. Each has something different to offer. Use the guide in the appendix to find the zoo that will best suit the needs and interests of your children. All help children understand the basic needs of organisms to live and thrive and allow children to observe animals in reproductions of their native environments.

The *Benchmarks for Science Literacy* of the American Association for the Advancement of Science suggests that all urban children should have the opportunity to observe a variety of animals at the zoo. Trips to the zoo help youngsters learn many of the core understandings in life science that are recommended for elementary school age children.

For instance, students in the early grades should know that some animals are alike in body form and behaviors, and others are very different from one another. They should understand that animals usually resemble their parents and that animals grow and change. They should begin to compare different animal life cycles.

Students should identify different body structures and their functions. For example, the teeth of mammals and reptiles and the beaks of birds are adapted to the foods that these animals eat. Carnivores can be expected to have sharp teeth or bills and sharp claws or talons adapted for hunting and eating prey. Herbivores usually have teeth adapted for grinding plant materials. The beaks of birds may be adapted to eating flowers, fruit, seeds or nuts, insects, fish or animals. Fish and reptiles too may be herbivores or carnivores.

Herbivores and carnivores differ in behaviors as well as body structures. Because plants are lower in nutrient value than the flesh of animals, herbivores may spend most of their waking hours browsing for food. When hunting is good, carnivores have more time for leisure. Big cats may spend much of the day sleeping. Herbivores are more likely than carnivores to live in large social groups. Pack hunting animals, such as hyenas and wolves, are social carnivores. Some animal behaviors, such as nest building, hibernation, and migration, are influenced by environmental conditions.

Different animals may have different structures for the same purpose—for example, the sharp teeth of predatory mammals or the sharp beaks of birds of prey mentioned above, or the very different wings of butterflies, birds, and bats. Children should be familiar with both the exoskeletons of insects and crustaceans and the boney skeletons of vertebrate animals including mammals, fish, birds, and reptiles. Protective shells may be made of calcium carbonate as in snail shells, bone and skin as in turtle shells, or tough hide as in armadillos.

Young children should learn that living things are found almost everywhere in the world. Students in early grades should look for ways in which animals in various habitats differ from one another. They should look for behaviors and physical characteristics that help animals in different habitats to survive. For example, animals adapted to live in cold environments may have thick fur, down, or layers of fat to insulate them against the cold. They may also have white fur to camouflage them in snowy landscapes. Animals adapted to live in open grasslands may have tawny fur to help them blend into the landscape and may be able to run fast. Animals that inhabit the treetops will have adaptations to help them jump and climb. They may also vocalize to stay in contact with others hidden in the leafy canopy. Animals that live in the water will have adaptations that help them to move through the water. Fish have fins and tails. Aquatic mammals have limbs like fins. For example, sea lions have flippers instead of front legs or arms and streamlined bodies that are better for moving through the water than on land. Penguins use their wings as flippers.

Older elementary school children should know that the features of animals can be used to sort them into groups. There are many different ways to group animals, such as by behaviors, habitats, or physical features.

Children in upper elementary school grades should understand that organisms interact with one another in various ways, providing food and shelter or competing for resources. All animals impact their environment, and some can change a habitat in extreme ways. For example, the dam building of beavers can transform a wooded area into a pond or meadow by flooding previously dry land. Because of their ability to transform the landscape, beavers are considered a keystone species. Keystone species are essential to the functioning of the entire community of living things of which they are a part.

Black-tailed prairie dogs are a keystone species of the prairie. Like beavers, they can be considered ecosystem engineers. They impact the prairie ecosystem in multiple ways. Their burrowing loosens the soil, increasing its ability to sustain plant life; their foraging enriches the soil and increases the plant diversity of the plains. This in turn increases the diversity of wildlife who graze in prairie dog colonies. Their burrows act as homes to other creatures. Black-tailed prairie dogs are a critical food source for the endangered black-footed ferret, swift fox, coyotes, hawks, eagles, and badgers. Several New York City zoos house prairie dog colonies to introduce children to these charming members of the squirrel family. Children should also know that human activities have a profound impact on ecosystems. Prairie dogs are a classic example of this. During the 20th century, most of the Great Plains has been converted to farming or pastureland and about 98 percent of all prairie dogs have been exterminated. They have been reduced to approximately 5% of their historic range.

In any environment, some kinds of plants and animals thrive, some will struggle to survive, and some will not survive at all. An exotic animal introduced into a new environment may not survive, or—like the introduced Norway rat, starling, pigeon, and house sparrow—it may thrive and out-compete native species.

Children should also understand that changes in an organism's habitat are sometimes beneficial and sometimes harmful. As our society confronts the question of how a warming planet will impact our lives, it is important to understand that some organisms will benefit from a warming planet, and many others will be harmed. For example, the polar bear is already threatened due to loss of its sea ice habitat.

New York Aquarium

Because of its extensive indoor exhibits, the New York Aquarium is an excellent place to visit when the weather is too cold, too hot, or too wet to be outdoors. But it is also a wonderful place to visit on a warm day when you can combine your visit with a trip to the beach. The aquarium is compact enough so that you can see almost everything in a whirlwind visit, but your visit will provide a deeper learning experience if you choose a theme to focus on, questions to explore, or specific creatures to observe. As always, it is best to offer children some choice about what to see and do.

Oceans cover almost 70 percent of the Earth's surface, and life began in the oceans. Ocean environments vary widely in temperature, pressure, and salinity. In addition, sunlight intensity diminishes with depth until the ocean depths are in perpetual darkness. Marine organisms have adapted to all of these environmental extremes. As a result, the aquarium is one of the best places in New York to observe the extremes of animal variation. You will find soft-bodied invertebrates such as sea jellies and hard-bodied invertebrates such as lobsters. Vertebrate marine animals include reptiles such as the sea turtle, birds such as the penguin, and mammals such as the California sea lion, as well as sharks and fish. There are sleek, limbless eels, five-pointed sea stars, and eight-armed octopuses. There are tiny shrimp and huge sharks. Sea creatures come in a rainbow of colors and patterns. Textures range from the rough and brittle sea stars, to leathery turtles, scaly fish, and gelatinous sea jellies.

Consider predator–prey relationships, food chains, and food webs. Discover a sea lion's role in the food web, and learn why sharks and other predators are essential to a balanced food chain. Compare and contrast the life cycles and family organization of sea creatures from sea jellies and sea horses to sea otters. Think about the role of communication in the undersea environment, where sound travels far and light conditions vary by the depth and clarity of the water. If you ask most children to name an animal, most will think of dogs and cats, or cows and chickens. The most familiar animals are mammals and birds, but only a small number of mammals and birds make their homes in the ocean. Observe adaptations to locomotion in the sea, from passive drifting to crawling and swimming. Notice how marine mammals have come to resemble fish in many ways. Consider how penguins seem to fly through the water with their flightless wings. Notice how these creatures have adapted to the ocean environment by becoming streamlined like fish. Also pay special attention to the huge diversity of invertebrates (animals without backbones) that make their homes in the sea. You might want to use the biodiversity worksheet in this book to help you keep track of the wide variety of creatures you encounter.

Exhibits at the aquarium are mostly organized by ocean environments. You will find reproductions of a wide variety of marine habitats, from shallow coastal shores to deep sea environments. Explore the Shore is a child's eye view of a typical local seashore. This hands-on coastal exhibit lets you get up close and personal with the underwater creatures living in a salt marsh as you peer down or through the glass-walled shallow water exhibit. Visitors can touch sea stars and horseshoe crabs in an open tank with the guidance of docents to ensure that both you and the creatures will feel safe and secure. A specially engineered glass hallway allows you to experience a 400-gallon wave crashing over you while you remain perfectly dry.

At Glover's Reef, you can observe the colorful schools of fish that swim above a coral reef without snorkeling or scuba diving. Compare these neon-bright fish to the drab stringrays that seem to fly above them and the moray eels that lurk in the crevices of the coral reef. The Glover's Reef and Conservation Hall exhibits will help you and your children explore human impacts on marine ecosystems. Globally, coral reefs are under threat from climate change as well as overuse of reef resources. Coral reefs are structures produced by living colonial invertebrate organisms that thrive only in marine waters containing few nutrients. These coral organisms secrete an exoskeleton of calcium carbonate. The accumulated skeletons from past generations of coral produce a limestone formation on which the living corals grow. These reefs support a great variety of other animal and plant life. High nutrient levels such as those found in runoff from agricultural areas can harm reefs. Ocean acidification threatens to dissolve the calcium carbonate of which coral reefs are made.

The Alien Stingers exhibit introduces the beautiful, fascinating, and often dangerous family of sea jellies. Sea jellies are an ancient and primitive form of life, closely related to corals and anemones. Touch screens throughout the halls allow visitors to play jelly games and learn jelly facts. Did you know that sea jellies metamorphose like butterflies? Learn about the fascinating complex life cycle of these remarkable creatures that float passively on the ocean currents.

The Sea Cliff exhibit is an outdoor 300-foot-long recreation of the rocky North Pacific coastline with an underwater viewing area inside. Here you can compare the body forms and behaviors of a variety of marine mammals including seals, otters, and walruses with penguins, the birds that fly through the water. In the deep-ocean Shark and Loggerhead Sea Turtle exhibit, you can observe a variety of sharks up close and personal. Compare reef sharks, nurse sharks, and sand tiger sharks with stingrays and sea turtles in a floor-to-ceiling tank that gets you eye-to-eye with a few of the ocean's top predators. The loggerhead sea turtle is able to swim a third of the way around the world—one of the longest migrations of any marine animal. The orange-brown color of its shell and upper body helps it stand out from the other six sea turtle species.

The New York Aquarium website (http://www.nyaquarium.com/) provides information about most of the animals that you will encounter on your visit. Spend some time planning your visit by doing research on the animals you will find. Find children's books about life in the sea to read together before your visit, or watch *Finding Nemo* together so that your child will be ready to recognize "old friends" when you visit.

Engage

Before My Visit to the Aquarium

Use words and pictures to show what kinds of animals you expect to find at the aquarium.

Before My Visit to the Aquarium

Write a story or poem about your favorite ocean creature.

○ **Engage**

NAME:

DATE:

LOCATION:

Before My Visit to the Aquarium

Write a story or poem about your favorite ocean creature.

○ **Explore**

My Visit to the Aquarium

Use words and pictures to describe the animals you found at the aquarium.
Draw some animals with hard bodies and some animals with soft bodies.

54

NAME:

DATE:

LOCATION:

My Visit to the Aquarium

Use words and pictures to describe the animals you found at the aquarium.
Draw some animals with hard bodies and some animals with soft bodies.

Comparing Living Things

Compare animals with hard bodies and animals with soft bodies.

List ways they are alike.

List ways they are different.

Animals with soft bodies	Animals with hard bodies

Explain

NAME:

DATE:

LOCATION:

Comparing Living Things

Find two aquatic animals that breathe air. List them below.

_____ | _____

How are they alike? Think of as many ways as you can.

How are they different? Think of as many ways as you can.

Explore

NAME:

DATE:

LOCATION:

My Aquarium Ecosystem Drawings

Draw one ecosystem that you see at the aquarium. Is it deep sea, shallow ocean, coastal, or freshwater? _____

Explore

NAME:

DATE:

LOCATION:

My Aquarium Ecosystem Drawings

Draw a different ecosystem that you see at the aquarium. Is it deep sea, shallow ocean, coastal, or freshwater? _____

Animal Adaptations

What are the living and nonliving things in this aquatic environment?

Living things (Biotic factors)	Nonliving things (Abiotic factors)

Expand

NAME:

DATE:

LOCATION:

Animal Adaptations

How have the animals you observed adapted to living in the water?

Living things (Biotic factors)	Nonliving things (Abiotic factors)

○ Evaluate

NAME:

DATE:

LOCATION:

The Most Interesting Things I Learned

What are the most interesting things you learned from your trip
to the aquarium?

Bronx Zoo

The Wildlife Conservation Society (WCS) was founded in 1895 as the New York Zoological Society. It was one of the first conservation organizations in the U.S. The Society began with three core goals: to advance wildlife conservation, promote the study of zoology, and create a first-class zoo. WCS is now the parent organization for the largest network of urban zoos in the United States. Scientists at the zoo conduct research both at the zoo and throughout the world on animal reproduction, nutrition, and welfare to preserve wildlife and wild places around the globe.

The Bronx Zoo is the original and largest of the WCS zoos, covering 265 acres and housing over 4,000 animals. The zoo is an excellent place to go to observe animal features and behavior in settings that recreate wild habitats from around the globe. Each habitat affords the opportunity to observe physical and behavioral adaptations to the environment and relationships between the plants and animals. Think about the role of communication in wildlife communities, both between members of the same species and across species boundaries. Consider predator–prey relationships, food chains, and food webs. Compare and contrast the life cycles and family organization of animals from fish and amphibians to mammals and birds.

Because the zoo is very large, and children have limited attention and energy, plan to focus on just one or two major exhibits for your visit. Plan to visit at least one indoor exhibit because you can be sure to see the animals up close. Indoor exhibits can extend your comfortable visit to the zoo when the weather is too cold, too hot, or too wet to be outdoors. Be sure to offer the children some choice about what to see. The zoo is organized so that the major concepts of animal interactions with the environment can be observed in almost every exhibit.

The Mouse House is a wonderful exhibit for very young children. It allows children to compare and contrast the physical characteristics of several closely related animals in a very small area. The Mouse House is home to rodents from six continents and a wide variety of habitats—including rainforest, meadow, swamp, and desert—providing an opportunity to compare habitats as well as physical characteristics. For example, you can compare adaptations for locomotion in kangaroo rats to those in flying squirrels. The exhibit also houses a few predators that dine on rodents, so the food chain can also be explored here.

Most major exhibits at the zoo are organized around a geographic theme. The new Madagascar! exhibit recreates the unique habitats of this isolated land. The plants and animals of the world's fourth largest island are found nowhere else on

Earth. In this exhibit, you will see baobob and octopus trees and unique forested deserts. Compare the physical features of reptiles such as the Nile crocodile, the Radiated tortoise, Henkel's leaf-tailed gecko, and the tree boa. Compare the Madagscar Hissing Cockroach to our own local variety. See colorful freshwater Marakely fish swimming in a limestone tsingy cave. Compare four different species of Madagascar lemurs. Discover the fossa, a predator that resembles a small cougar, but is surprisingly not a member of the cat family.

The Bronx Zoo is the only metropolitan area zoo that still houses the large predatory cats, among the most exciting of all animals to observe. The African Plains exhibit recreates the African savanna. It provides the opportunity to view lions and other savanna dwellers, including storks, zebras, giraffes, gazelles, and African wild dogs. The Tiger Mountain exhibit recreates the Russian Far East woodlands, home to Siberian tigers. Animal behaviors can be observed at the daily tiger enrichment sessions, when keepers work with the cats to stimulate their curiosity and natural instincts. Keepers also teach the tigers behaviors that facilitate their care. At these sessions, observers have the chance to ask the keepers questions. This is a good chance to find out more about working with animals in the zoo.

Several exhibits allow visitors to compare and contrast the habitats, behaviors, and physical characteristics of a wide variety of primates and the plants and animals with which they interact in the wild. Exhibits recreate habitats from Asia, Africa, and the New World.

JungleWorld is an indoor re-creation of four types of Asian rainforest habitats. JungleWorld has troops of binturongs and silvered and ebony langurs. White-cheeked gibbons swing through the canopy above a Malayan tapir and black leopards, allowing children to directly compare the characteristics of mammals from different animal families. Look for adaptations for locomotion and camouflage and behaviors such as foraging for food. Compare and contrast the adaptations of predator and prey animals.

The Congo Gorilla Forest is a 6.5-acre recreation of the African rainforest that is home to more than twenty western lowland gorillas. The exhibit provides the opportunity for children to compare variations in physical characteristics among members of the primate family. Compare gorillas with colobus monkeys, marmosets, and mandrills.

The Gelada baboon exhibit is a recreation of the Ethiopian highlands. It is another great place to observe animal social interactions. The Gelada baboons in this exhibit use visual signals and vocalizations to communicate with one another. In the same exhibit, you can also observe a colony of rock hyraxes. This small, furry mammal looks like a large squirrel with no tail. Hyraxes vocalize with twitters, growls, whistles, and shrieks. This exhibit provides a good opportunity to compare and contrast the behaviors of two very different social mammals.

The Monkey House is another exhibit that can allow young people to observe primate behaviors and compare and contrast physical characteristics. The small primates in this exhibit are known as New World monkeys because they are native to the forests of South and Central America.

The Wildlife Conservation Society website (http://www.wcs.org/) provides information about most of the animals that you will encounter at the zoo. Spend some time planning your visit by doing research on the animals you will find and choosing those you are most interested in meeting face-to-face. Use the interactive Trip Planner to plan your route: http://tripplanner.bronxzoo.com/.

Central Park Zoo

The Central Park Zoo is located at 64th Street and Fifth Avenue in Manhattan, New York. It is compact, centrally located, and easily accessible by mass transit. It is easy to visit with young children and those with limited mobility, and is an especially good choice for those with limited time.

The Central Park Zoo began in 1864 as the Central Park Menagerie. In 1980, the Wildlife Conservation Society entered into an agreement with the City of New York to renovate and operate the zoo on behalf of the Parks Department. The new Central Park Zoo, now designed with a focus on the benefit of the animals, was re-opened to the public in 1985. It is an excellent place to observe animal features and behavior in settings that recreate wild habitats from around the globe. Each habitat will afford the opportunity to observe physical and behavioral adaptations to the environment and relationships between the plants and animals. The Tish Children's Zoo features a barnyard of friendly animals and places for little ones to scramble safely.

At the heart of the park, the sea lions bark a greeting to visitors as they have since the opening of the zoo. Sea lions are social creatures and excellent candidates for observing social interactions with an ethogram. Watch the keepers feed the sea lions and learn about marine mammal food chains and careers in wildlife conservation.

The arctic habitat of polar bears and the Antarctic turf of penguins and puffins are recreated at the Central Park Zoo. The endangered polar bear's thick layers of blubber and dense, waterproof fur help it survive the harsh Arctic winter. The indoor bird colony and outdoor polar bear pool allow close encounters with these cold-adapted creatures.

Animals that live in temperate regions must adapt to changing seasons. Animals from the temperate zones, including snow monkeys and red pandas, can be found along the temperate trail. It is a special treat to observe the snow monkeys on a snowy winter day.

Animals from tropical climates can be viewed in the Tropic Zone, a rainforest exhibit. Viewing platforms at various levels help you observe the animal life in all layers of the rainforest. Observe the variety of animal families found in the tropics; reptiles are represented by tortoises that creep slowly underfoot, and an unfamiliar mammal, the two-toed sloth, hangs from vines. These creatures have in common that they are very slow moving. How do they survive? Noisy hornbills call in the canopy. How are these birds similar to our familiar North American birds? How are they different? How does the large bill of the hornbill help it to survive?

The new Snow Leopard Exhibit recreates the mountains of central Asia. This exhibit exemplifies the WCS's commitment to the world's endangered animals. Only a few thousand of these cats remain in the wild. These snow leopards are a part of the Species Survival Program, which maintains populations of endangered species in zoos. Compare the snow leopard to the more familiar big cats. How do their different coat colorations help them to survive? Encourage your child to draw snow leopards, lions, and tigers in their natural habitats.

The Central Park Zoo is one of the best locations for conducting detailed observations of animal behavior. Consider completing the ethogram activity on a visit to this zoological park. Social sea lions, snow monkeys, and penguins are good candidates for this activity. It is also an excellent place to compare and contrast animal adaptations to a variety of climates. Use the graphic organizers provided to structure your observations.

Central Park Zoo visit planning notes:

Prospect Park Zoo

Like the other smaller zoological parks in New York City, the Prospect Park Zoo is now operated as part of the Wildlife Conservation Society and shares its mission to study and protect wildlife and to educate the public. It is situated on 12 acres nestled in a corner of Brooklyn's Prospect Park. The zoo can be entered from Flatbush Avenue within a relatively short walk from public transportation. It is possible to see the entire zoo on a single visit and be assured of seeing the animals up close, making it an especially good choice for younger children. This zoo features indoor exhibits that can make the zoo a good place to visit even if the weather isn't ideal. Even though the zoo is relatively small, children have limited attention and energy, so you should plan to focus on just one or two exhibits for your visit, then let the children follow their own interests.

The history of Prospect Park Zoo dates back to the late 1800s, when it began as a small menagerie operated by Prospect Park at a time when Brooklyn was an independent city. In 1896, the collection included a buffalo, three bears, a puma, two raccoons, and one eagle, along with an assortment of domestic animals that were likely to have been equally unfamiliar to the residents of the City of Brooklyn. This collection of animals was formalized as the Prospect Park Zoo in 1935. Evolving understanding about the needs of animals in captivity eventually made the old Prospect Park Zoo obsolete. The Wildlife Conservation Society took on the renovation and management of a new zoo in Prospect Park, which opened in 1993. Some architectural elements of the old zoo were saved, such as the domed elephant house, but bars, cages, and pits were replaced with naturalistic habitat exhibits. Larger animals such as elephants, giraffes, polar bears, and big cats were moved to the Bronx campus or relocated to other zoos better suited to their needs. Among the fiercest predators at the Prospect Park Zoo today are the house-cat size Pallas cat of the steppes of central Asia and the tiny Scops owl of Africa.

The Prospect Park Zoo features smaller animals such prairie dogs, river otters, meercats, and Hamadryas baboons. Among the largest animals are the gentle giant California sea lions. Many of these animals have in common that they live in extended social groups and pursue active social lives, making them easy for children to identify with. Many are known for their playful natures. Even though the Prospect Park Zoo is compact, it includes animals from the major families, including mammals, reptiles, birds, and amphibians.

Although the major life science concepts of animal life cycles, food chains and webs, adaptations, and interactions with the environment can be observed in almost every exhibit, this zoo is especially suited for observing, comparing, and contrasting animal behaviors, especially those in social groups. The science of animal behavior is called *ethology*. If animal behavior interests you, consider using the *ethogram* trip sheets to help you observe animal behavior like a naturalist.

How Do Animals Communicate?

Do they use sound, touch, or visual cues? What do they communicate about? Often predator–prey relationships can be explored in the context of communication. Courtship, mating, and raising young often involve communication. Compare the communication in the prairie dog village to the Hamadryas baboon colony. Older children might be interested in comparing the behaviors of the Hamadryas baboons to those of the Gelada baboons of the Ethiopian highlands, which can be found at the Bronx Zoo.

The zoo houses a wide variety of North American natives, such as the North American river otter, porcupine, and prairie dog, making it an excellent destination for children to study temperate forests ecosystems or American history. You may even encounter local wildlife at the zoo, including wild heron, bullfrogs, turtles, and ducks, as well as domestic farm animals such as sheep, goats, alpacas, and miniature horses on the "farm."

Some exhibits feature animal groups from far away with animals from every continent. You will find Australian kangaroos and wallabies and emus, African baboons, and South American monkeys.

Compare Animal Behaviors

Inside the aviary you will find exotic birds such as rose-breasted cockatoos, peacocks, and mynahs. In springtime, compare the strutting peacocks to native pigeons strutting during courting.

Animal architecture is another common theme at the Prospect Park Zoo. You can compare porcupine dens—which may be constructed in caves, hollow logs, burrows, snow banks, or on tree branches—to prairie dog or river otter burrows. You may also be able to compare duck nests to cockatoo nests. Exhibits encourage young visitors to role-play animal behaviors. They can climb a spider's web, burrow through the prairie dog town, or climb in a giant duck's nest.

Where do animals hang out? Are they found on the ground? In trees? In the water? How much time do they spend in different parts of their habitats? Does this change at various times of the day? Do older animals behave differently? Do males and females behave the same? What other questions about animal behavior do you have?

Adaptable or Highly Adapted?

Some animals, such as the North American porcupines, are highly adaptable and can live in a wide range of habitats including tundra, rangeland, and desert, in addition to their preferred woodland habitats. Others, such as the red panda, are highly adapted to a particular environment. Red pandas are found only in high altitude temperate bamboo forests of Asia.

What's for Dinner?

Many of the zoo residents are herbivores, but some are picky eaters and some are not. This is another way to think about whether an animal is adaptable or highly adapted. Porcupines, for instance, eat buds, roots, stems, leaves, berries, and nuts during spring and summer, and turn to evergreen needles and tree bark in winter. Hamadryas baboons also eat a wide variety of foods, including grass, roots, tubers, nuts, insects, eggs, and small birds and mammals. Like porcupines, they change their diet depending on what is easiest to get at a given time. These animals are highly adaptable. If one food source becomes scarce, they can adapt by eating another food. Can red panda do this? What other animals are highly adapted? Which other animals are highly adaptable?

Day or Night?

Some creatures, such as owls, are strictly nocturnal. Others, such as the porcupine, are mainly nocturnal, but sometimes forage during the day. Learn about the creatures that wake up when we go to sleep.

The Prospect Park Zoo is planning renovations in the near future, so be alert to the possibility that exhibits may be closed. Be sure to check the website (http://www.prospectparkzoo.com/) for up-to-date information on exhibits. As always, advance planning will make your visit more successful.

Prospect Park Wildlife Center visit planning notes:

Staten Island Zoo

The Staten Island Zoo is currently the only zoo in New York City independent of the Wildlife Conservation Society. It was the first zoo in the country to specifically dedicate itself to fulfilling an educational mission. With its small size, it has much in common with the Central Park and Prospect Park Zoos. The Staten Island Zoological Society has followed these goals since its inception:

- To disseminate a knowledge of zoology and an appreciation of animal life,

- To maintain a zoological garden where small mammals, birds, reptiles, amphibians, and tropical fish will be on display for observation and study,

- Through local facilities, accessible to all of Staten Island, instill in children an understanding and appreciation of living creatures,

- To provide lectures and facilities for group meetings devoted to the study of natural history.

What to Do at the Zoo

The major life science concepts of animal life cycles, food chains and webs, adaptations, and interactions with the environment can be observed in almost every exhibit. This zoo is especially suited for observing, comparing, and contrasting animal behaviors. For example, compare the behaviors of solitary cats to social meerkats, aquatic otters to terrestrial prairie dogs, and cold-blooded snakes and insects to warm-blooded birds and mammals.

This zoo also offers the opportunity to compare an open grassland ecosystem to a tropical rainforest ecosystem.

A Focus on Snakes and Other Reptiles

This small zoo has earned an international reputation for its reptile collection. It has one of the most extensive collections of North American rattlesnakes in the world as well as snakes from around the world, including pythons and anacondas. This collection makes the zoo worthwhile for older children to visit, just for the opportunity to explore reptiles in depth. The reptile exhibit aims to use increased knowledge to reduce fear of snakes. The zoo has recently completed major renovations to the reptile exhibit. The new exhibit includes native reptiles and reptiles from around the world, including alligators and turtles.

How Many Legs Does It Have?

Young children will benefit from simply exploring the wide variety of animals at this zoo that do not have any legs. They can also focus on animals without fur or feathers. Once your child recognizes the features of snakes and turtles in this exhibit, have them look for other reptiles in the other exhibits at the zoo.

Does It Have Fur, Feathers, or Scales?

The reptile wing also houses lizards and frogs in naturalistic settings, reproducing their native habitats. There is also a collection of invertebrates. For all children, this zoo provides an excellent opportunity to easily compare and contrast physical features of reptiles, amphibians, birds, and fish with the more familiar mammals.

The Staten Island Zoo allows the opportunity to compare animals from different ecosystems in a compact one-building setting. They can compare the wild animals in the main building with farm animals in the Children's Center Children or the Clydesdale barn and the petting zoo.

Some animals are alike in physical features and behaviors, and others are very different from one another

The zoo's new African Savannah exhibit allows children to observe the animals native to the vast grasslands of central and southern Africa in a realistic representation of the African plains. The exhibits allow children to observe animals in naturalistic settings, showing how the animals live and interact in the wild. This exhibit includes larger animals such as leopards and antelopes, in addition to the smaller mandrills, lizards, and meerkats.

The Tropical Forest exhibit represents an endangered South American tropical forest with both flora and fauna of this ecosystem. Invertebrates found in different habitats around the world are also housed in this exhibit.

There are many different ways to group animals, such as by behaviors, habitats or physical features

The prairie dog and otter exhibits provide the opportunity to observe social animal behaviors up close. The otters can be observed either below the water or out in the open air.

The Staten Island Zoo houses an exceptional assortment of wildcats. The bobcat exhibit allows the visitors to safely observe bobcats jumping and climbing in their naturalistic enclosure. Compare the bobcat to the serval and to the ocelots housed in the Tropical Rainforest exhibit. Can you find other big cats in this zoo? What other kinds of cats do you know about? How are these animals alike in physical features and behaviors and how are they different? How are their environments the same and how are they different? What makes a cat, a cat?

With a focus on feathered creatures, you can compare the emus and peacocks in outdoor enclosures to the starlings and shrikes in the African Savannah exhibit. Do any of these exotic birds look like wild birds living in New York City?

From sharks to shrimps, the aquarium allows observation of aquatic animals from around the world.

Staten Island Zoo visit planning notes:

Engage

NAME:

DATE:

LOCATION:

Before My Visit to the Zoo

Use words and pictures to show what kinds of animals you expect to find at the zoo.

Engage—cont.

NAME:

DATE:

LOCATION:

Before My Visit to the Zoo

What do you wonder about animals at the zoo?
What do you hope to discover on your trip to the zoo?

NAME:

DATE:

LOCATION:

Before My Visit to the Zoo

Write a story or poem about your favorite wild animal.

 **Explore**

NAME:

DATE:

LOCATION:

My Visit to the Zoo
Use words and pictures to describe an animal you found at the zoo.

76

Explore

NAME:

DATE:

LOCATION:

My Visit to the Zoo

Use words and pictures to describe another animal you found at the zoo.

NAME:

DATE:

LOCATION:

My Visit to the Zoo

Use words and pictures to describe another animal you found at the zoo.

Explore

NAME:

DATE:

LOCATION:

Comparing Living Things

Fur, feathers, scales, and skin.
Draw an animal with each.

Animal with fur	Animal with feathers
Animal with scales	Animal with skin

○ **Explain**

NAME:

DATE:

LOCATION:

Comparing Living Things

Find a carnivore and an herbivore. List them below.

_____	_____

How are they alike? Think of as many ways as you can.

How are they different? Think of as many ways as you can.

Explore

My Ecosystem Drawings

Draw one ecosystem that you see at the zoo. Where in the world is it?_____

Explain

Comparing Living and Nonliving Things

List the living and nonliving things in this environment.

Living things	Nonliving things

 # **Explain**

Animal Adaptations

How has one animal you observed adapted to living in this environment?

Animal _____

Adaptation (example: long ears, striped fur)

How does the adaptation help this animal survive in its environment?

Evaluate

NAME:

DATE:

LOCATION:

Animal Adaptations
How have human activities hurt this animal in the wild?
Animal _____
Human activity
How does the human activity hurt the animal in its environment?
What can be done to help solve this problem?

Evaluate

NAME:

DATE:

LOCATION:

The Most Interesting Things I Learned

What are the most interesting things you learned from your trip to the zoo?

⊸ **Engage**

Ethogram of Animal Behavior

- Choose an animal that interests you and observe it for a few minutes.

The animal that I observed was a _____.
I observed this animal at _____
(location) on _____ (date) at _____ (time).
The weather was _____.

- Identify an interesting behavior that you observe. Describe the behavior below. Explain why you thought this behavior was interesting.

Explore

NAME:

DATE:

LOCATION:

Ethogram of Animal Behavior

- Choose another animal to compare to the first one. Describe the two animals do you want to compare.

- How are they alike? How are they different?

- Explain why you think it would be interesting to compare the two animals.

The first animal that I observed was _____.

The second animal that I observed was _____.

- What difference do you expect to see between the two animals? Why?

Expand

NAME:

DATE:

LOCATION:

Data Chart for Ethogram of Animal Behavior				
Collect your data. Count the number of times the animals perform the observed behavior in two, minute intervals. (If you are working alone, you can alternate collecting data from each animal.)				
	First Animal		Second Animal	
Time Interval	Tally the number of times the behavior was observed	Total number	Tally the number of times the behavior was observed	Total number
0–2 minutes				
2–4 minutes				
4–6 minutes				
6–8 minutes				
8–10 minutes				
10–12 minutes				
12–14 minutes				
14–16 minutes				
16–18 minutes				

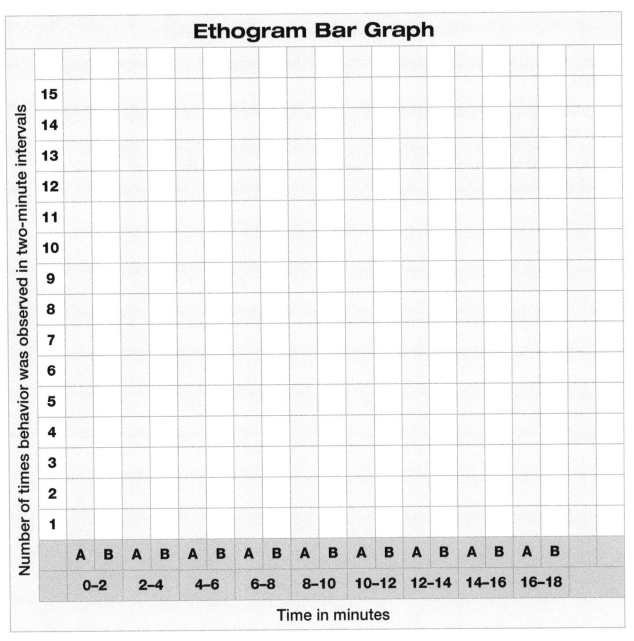

Ethogram Bar Graph

Number of times behavior was observed in two-minute intervals

	15																	
	14																	
	13																	
	12																	
	11																	
	10																	
	9																	
	8																	
	7																	
	6																	
	5																	
	4																	
	3																	
	2																	
	1																	
	A	B	A	B	A	B	A	B	A	B	A	B	A	B	A	B	A	B
	0–2		2–4		4–6		6–8		8–10		10–12		12–14		14–16		16–18	

Time in minutes

Evaluate

NAME:

DATE:

LOCATION:

Analysis of Animal Behavior

Describe the results of your ethogram here. Do you notice any patterns?

Did you expect these results? Is your hypothesis supported by the data?

What else would you like to find out about how these animals behave?

Botanic Gardens and Farms

Brooklyn Botanic Garden

According to the *Benchmarks for Science Literacy*, urban children should have the opportunity to observe a variety of plants in their neighborhood and gardens. Primary grade students should know that:

- Plants are found almost everywhere in the world.
- Plants are often different in different places.
- Some plants are similar but others are very different from one another.
- Some plants have similar needs for water, sun, and soil and others differ.

In all seasons and weather, students can actively explore plants from major ecosystems of the world in the indoor Steinhardt Conservatory. The outdoor collections include ornamental plants from around the world that can thrive in our local temperate climate. Native plant systems can be observed in the local flora garden. Students should also know that the features of plants can be used to sort them into groups. The Botanic Garden groups plants by climate, local habitat, and plant family.

Upper elementary grade students know that some fossil organisms are similar to existing organisms, but some are quite different. In the Steinhardt Conservatory, the Trail of Evolution traces the development of plant life from its origin four billion years ago to the present day with both plant specimens and real and replicated fossils.

To the right of the Trail of Evolution is the Aquatic House. With a variety of tropical and subtropical aquatic plants from around the world displayed in a naturalistic swamp environment, this exhibit demonstrates the range of physical adaptations that plants have made to live in, on, and near water.

By the end of the 5th grade, students should know that in any environment, some kinds of plants thrive, some will struggle to survive, and some will not survive at all. Adaptations help plant to survive in different environments.

Major Ecosystems of the World

Plants of the tropical rainforests differ from plants of the deserts. All land plants need water, sun, and soil. Ecosystems around the world vary in average annual temperatures as well as seasonal variations and extremes. They vary in rainfall and soil type. The Steinhardt Conservatory allows students to observe and compare plant adaptations to different climates.

The Warm Temperate Pavilion exhibits the diversity of plant life in warm temperate regions around the world. Familiar examples of warm temperate climates are the Mediterranean Basin and coastal regions of California. This climate is characterized by cool, wet winters and hot, dry summers, which periodically result in fire. The temperature range is generally between 45 and 55 degrees Fahrenheit in winter and 70 and 85 degrees Fahrenheit in summer. The air is often foggy along coastlines. Plants in these climate zones have special adaptations that allow them to survive drought. They may have small, fine leaves or hairy leaves that help conserve water. Hairy leaves also capture water droplets from fog. Some, such as the Mediterranean olive tree, have silver leaves, which reflect light and protect from too much sun. There are other invisible adaptations underground such as corms, rhizomes, tubers, or bulbs, which store nutrients while plants are dormant during the dry season.

Compare the plants of the warm temperate zone to the consistently moist environment of the tropics of the Amazon basin, African rainforest, and eastern Asia in the Tropical Pavilion. This exhibit features economically important plants used for fragrance, food, medicine, and industry, as well as ornamental plants, showing that humans are among the animals depending on plants. This exhibit emphasizes the dangers of habitat loss in the world's tropical forests.

The Desert Pavilion houses plants from arid regions in both the Old and New World and provides the opportunity to closely observe a wide variety of plant adaptations to extremely dry habitats.

Local Ecosystems

Outside, the Native Flora Garden lets you take a trip back in time to observe the local ecosystem before the growth of the city. In just over two acres, it includes nine distinct plant communities found within a 100-mile radius of New York City: serpentine rock, dry meadow, kettle pond, bog, pine barrens, wet meadow and stream, deciduous woodland, limestone ledge, and coniferous forests. All plants in this garden are adapted to distinct ecological niches, determined by environmental factors such as topography, geology, soil acidity or alkalinity, moisture, drainage, and light.

Children should understand that changes in an organism's habitat are sometimes beneficial and sometimes harmful. Urbanization is an extreme example of changes to an environment caused by human activity. The native flora garden provides a glimpse of what the New York region looked like before European settlers arrived and the process of urbanization began.

The serpentine area of the native flora garden can help children understand how certain species are better adapted than others to a specific habitat. Serpentine, a greenish rock with a high magnesium content, is found primarily on Staten Island.

Serpentine habitat is extremely arid, nutrient-poor, and prone to fire, with toxic levels of elements such as chromium in the soil that inhibit the growth of many plants. Serpentine creates a stunted forest-and-savannah-like plant community. Only a limited number of trees, ferns, and wildflowers can thrive in this ecosystem, differing from the rest of the region only in the underlying rock.

Another habitat defined by the underlying rock is the limestone area. Limestone areas are composed of sedimentary rock, usually limestone or marble, and are as alkaline as peat bogs are acidic. Plants in these areas are adapted to the highly alkaline (high pH) conditions.

The dry meadow has thin, infertile, sandy soil. Dry meadows are open areas with mostly herbaceous plants and few trees and shrubs. The roots of grasses are adapted to withstand alternating conditions of drought and dampness. Flowering plants thrive in the meadow, including milkweed and butterfly weed, which attract bees, beetles, flies, wasps, and butterflies. You will also find the common native wildflowers goldenrod and New England and New York asters.

Kettle ponds are found throughout Long Island, formed from giant boulders of ice from the last ice age. Although they may dry out in winter or during a drought, kettle ponds quickly fill with the first rains. Plants that tolerate periodic flooding thrive here, such as ferns and blue flag iris, jewelweed and ironweed, and shrubs such as bayberry and dogwood.

The kettle ponds support frogs, dragonflies, and mosquitoes. Birds are attracted to the area by insect activity. The dense growth of cattail causes the pond to gradually fill in and become a marsh, an example of how a plant can cause a habitat to change over a period of many years.

The bog is one of the most unusual native habitats. The spongy material under the bog is actually not soil, but an accumulation of plant debris resulting from the acidic, anaerobic conditions preventing old growth from decomposing. Bogs are the natural home of most insectivorous plants. These plants have adapted to living in the nutrient-poor bog with a variety of ways to entrap and digest insects. Acid-loving shrubs of the laurel family grow in bogs. Other bog plants include the sweet pepperbush and the cranberry. Eventually, enough peat accumulates for moisture and acid tolerant trees to grow.

Pine-barren soil is sandy, poor in nutrients, and relatively acidic. The trees most suited to this unusual environment are pitch pine, scrub oak, and blackjack oak. Blueberries, huckleberries, and hollies thrive here. You will also find native prickly pear cactus. Most of the trees native to the pine barrens are well adapted to the periodic fires that commonly occur there. These fires help to rejuvenate the forest, clearing the land of accumulated organic debris and stimulating new growth. Pitch pine is highly adapted to periodic fire. Fire is essential to renew the pitch pine forest. It is required for the cones to open, releasing seeds for the growth of new plants.

A third moist area is the wet meadow. Wet meadow plants may also grow along the course of a stream, or where seepage water accumulates at the bottom of a hill or along a wet ditch. In the Native Flora Garden, the wet meadow is fed by a slow-flowing stream. The organic matter and silt carried by streams enriches the soil of the wet meadow. Sedges, grasses, and rushes in particular thrive here. Compare the wet meadow to the dry meadow.

In the woodland section of the Native Flora Garden you can see a typical Northeast deciduous forest. This is the natural terrestrial plant community of the region. Most of the native woodland trees are oaks, maples, hickories, walnuts, beeches, and sweet gum. Another distinctive native tree is the sassafras, with its one-, two-, or three-lobed leaves that look like mittens. Below the trees is an understory of native rhododendron and mountain laurels. The woodland floor is covered with wildflowers, which bloom in early spring to take advantage of the sunlight that reaches the ground before tree leaves develop.

Along the border are evergreen coniferous trees found in the forests to the north or up in the mountains: Canadian hemlocks, junipers (eastern red cedars), and eastern white pines. What needles do fall discourage growth of plants in the understory.

Plant Family Collections

Most of us can recognize animal families, such as the cats, snakes, or crustaceans, but we are less familiar with plant families unless we are gardeners. The plant family collections organize plants by their evolutionary relationships, usually defined by reproductive strategies.

For example, most of the earliest plants reproduced from spores, not seeds. Seeds contain a miniature plant ready to sprout, whereas spores are simple, single-celled reproductive structures. The first plants were algae; from them, terrestrial plants originated. Among these primitive plants are the ferns. All of these primitive plants are confined to damp and shady areas, because their reproductive cycle requires water. You can find ferns growing south of the Japanese pond.

Flowering plants are divided into two main groups: the monocots and the dicots. Monocots have one cotyledon (the first leaf produced on a seedling) and leaves with parallel veins. The flowers usually have three or six petals. In the Monocot Border, you can find examples of monocots with large colorful flowers such as lilies and cannas, as well as grasses with simple, often inconspicuous green flowers.

As their name suggests, dicotyledons have two cotyledons, or first seedling leaves. These plants also have net-veined leaves. Their flower parts come in fours or fives or multiples of four or five. Dicots are much more diverse than monocots.

Nearby the ferns are the conifers or cone-producing plants: pines, junipers, cypresses, and so forth.

Plants can depend on wind, water, or animals to carry their pollen to other plants or to disperse their seeds. Children may enjoy going on a seed hunt in the botanic garden and comparing the different shapes and sizes that seeds come in. How do the seeds travel to a good place to sprout?

Science Safaris in New York City

New York Botanical Garden

In 1891, land in the northern Bronx was set aside by the New York State Legislature for the "creation of a garden of the highest class for the City of New York." The inspiration for the garden came from a visit to the Royal Botanical Garden in England by members of the Torrey Botanical Club, who immediately envisioned such a magnificent garden in New York City.

Today, the garden is a National Historic Landmark and is situated on 250 acres that includes natural features such as waterfalls, the Bronx River, rocky outcrops, and ponds. A living museum, the garden has more than 1 million plants in its fifty gardens and collections. Two recent additions to the garden include the Nolen Greenhouses for Living Collections and the Home Gardening Center. The Nolen Greenhouses is a behind-the-scenes structure that provides much-needed growing space for many of the garden's delicate plants. It has eight growing zones that allow for the growth and care of plants from the different climates of the world. The Nolan Greenhouses is also the site of much of the scientific research that occurs in the garden. Many of the orchids, bulbs, and perennial plants that you see throughout the garden have had their start here! The Home Gardening Center was designed with the hobbyist gardener in mind. It contains a number of smaller gardens, including a Vegetable Garden and a Garden for the Senses that demonstrate models of gardens and offers suggestions of plants that you could reproduce at home or in a school garden. The Plant Trials Garden displays annuals, perennials, bulbs, and shrubs that are suited to our local climate.

The Enid A. Haupt Conservatory—the iconic Victorian-era glass structure—is a New York City Landmark. It opened in 1902 and houses the World of Plants exhibit. Described as a "permanent ecotour of the world," this exhibit includes a tropical rainforest, deserts, aquatic plants, and a both noteworthy and extensive collection of palm trees. Visit the conservatory to observe how plants are adapted to live in different climates and ecosystems. Children may also recognize plants from countries where their families come from or places that they have visited.

Step back in time and walk through New York City before colonial times. The Forest is a 50-acre space that is the largest remaining stand of the native forest that once covered New York City. You will encounter some trees that are over 200 years old! The Bronx River runs through this area and creates a natural waterfall. The Forest is a great place to do phenology—the study of the timing of seasonal biological events. Green-up is the biological changes that indicate the beginning of the growing season for plants. Children could note what happens during the different seasons and discuss how our local plants are adapted to the changing seasons. Children could also collect and observe leaves and seeds to determine the diversity of trees in the forest. (Remember to leave your collections in the forest so that they can continue to be a part of the ecosystem!)

Children both young and old will enjoy visiting the Everett Children's Adventure Garden. It is an interactive, hands-on, kinesthetic space designed for children to explore the wonders of nature. Look at the large flower models—challenge children to notice and identify these parts in the real flowers in the garden. There is also a touch tank where children can play with and learn about aquatic plants and an indoor space with microscopes that allow for a closer look.

The New York Botanical Garden is a great place to visit year-round. The different outdoor gardens, such as the Lilac, Tulips, and Peony gardens, offer beautifully colored blooms in the spring and early summer. The Ross Conifer Arboretum displays spruces, pines, and firs from around the globe; some of them were planted in the early 1900s! This is a great place to learn about global tree diversity. In the fall, the Chrysanthemum Garden is in full bloom with colors that mirror the foliage of the trees. When planning your visit, check out the website (http://www.nybg.org/) to see what is in bloom. The Home Gardening Center and Children's Garden offer demonstrations and family fun events that are posted on the website.

New York Botanical Garden visit planning notes:

Queens Botanical Garden

The tag line of the Queens Botanical Garden is "where people, plants and cultures meet." Located in highly diverse Flushing, NY, the Queens Botanical Garden is committed to "presenting plants as an expression of cultural traditions."

With no entry fees, visitors freely walk through the entrance that is graced by a sculpture of an American Hornbeam tree and flanked by two Blue Atlas Cedars that were a part of the original 1939 garden! QBG grew out a 1939 World's Fair exhibit called Gardens on Parade. To make room for the 1964-65 World's Fair, the Queens Botanical Garden was moved, along with a number of signature plants, to a 39-acre site within the Kissena Park Corridor and was considered an open space legacy of that fair. The Queens Botanical Garden is currently in the midst of enacting a 2001 master plan that is based on principles of sustainability and the expression of cultural diversity.

The Visitor and Administrator Center is a platinum certified LEED© (Leadership in Energy and Environmental Design) building. It has key features such as a bioswale, sun shades, a green roof, and composting toilets all designed to conserve energy and water. A bioswale is a low-lying planted area that is especially designed to manage storm-water and keep it from entering New York City's wastewater system. The green roof not only provides a habitat for insects and birds, but it also insulates the building and prevents storm-water runoff. Visit www.queensbotanical.org/media/file/QBG.swf to learn more about the features of this building. Children could also see how much energy is generated by the building's solar power system and saved by the geothermal system.

Plants used on and around the building are native species—plants that have evolved and are especially adapted to live in our local environment. To keep plants around the garden healthy and to reduce the amount of synthetic pesticides, the Garden incorporates Integrated Pest Management, which leverages the natural interdependence of organisms in an ecosystem.

Visit the different gardens to learn about plant adaptations and characteristics. The Plants in Community garden displays plants that are native to New York. They are arranged according to their botanical families. Although the scientific names may be difficult for small children to remember (*Asclepiadaceae, Berberidaceae, Compositae, Fabaceae, Liliaceae, Polypodiaceae,* and *Rosaceae*), children could observe these family groups to learn about what characteristics are used to classify plants. For water management, there is a system of bioswales and cleansing biotopes (native wetland species that cleanse water) throughout the garden. Children could also visit a meadow of wildflowers and grasses that are allowed to grow to mature height.

The meadow is a great place to observe the interactions between birds, insects, and plants. The Bee Garden is popular with education classes and features plants that attract bees and flavor honey. The herb garden features herbs that are significant in Asian and Native American cultures.

The Queens Botanical Garden has an extensive menu of school programs that explore the collections of the garden. Visit www.queensbotanical.org to learn more. The website also has information about their composting program—you could visit the Composting Demonstration Garden and learn how to compost in your home or classroom.

Queens Botanic Garden visit planning notes:

Queens County Farm Museum

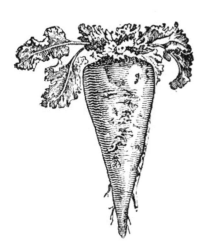

New York City's only working historic farm, the Queens County Farm Museum is located on 47 acres of land and has been an active farm since 1697. This makes it the longest continuously farmed site in the state. The western half of the historic farmhouse was built by the original landowners in 1772 (and restored in 1986). The eastern half of the house was added in the 1800s. The farm has since passed through many owners, the most notable being the Creedmoor State Hospital from 1926–1975. The farm was used as a rehabilitation site for patients, who grew produce for the hospital's kitchen and flowers to decorate the hospital grounds.

Today, the Queens County Farm Museum is owned by the Department of Parks and has been designated a New York City Landmark since 1975. With the current farm-to-table movement in foods, a visit to the Queens Farm is a great way to connect children to the agricultural past of much of New York City and give them a first-hand experience with the origins of their food.

Young children could visit the farm to learn about the characteristics of common farm animals and observe how animals grow and change. Older children could ask questions about selective breeding, adaptations, and heredity. The farm has mainly "heritage breeds." These are animals with a genetic history, and many of them are in danger of becoming extinct. Although they are hardy—they thrive in natural environments—they do not do so well on modern large-scale farms. It is a goal of the farm to conserve these heritage breeds for future generations. For example, you could see a Gloucester Old Spots-mix pig. It is also called an orchard pig because it loves to eat fallen fruit and does not dig or kill the roots of fruit trees. This breed of pig is listed as critical on the American Livestock Breeds Conservancy list. Children can also see a Cotswold sheep, one of the oldest wool breeds in the world.

The farm practices sustainable agriculture, using crop rotation instead of pesticides and developing pasture-based systems for their animals. All of the farm's produce—herbs, honey, eggs, and vegetables—travel no more than 15 miles to markets or restaurants. Children can visit beehives, a chicken coop, an orchard, and planting fields among other interesting sites on this working farm. It is a great way to learn about the interdependence between humans and other living things. Visit the website (http://www.queensfarm.org/) when you are ready to plan your visit. There are year-round activities for families and special programs for school groups.

⊸ **Engage**

My Favorite Plant or Flower

Do you have a favorite plant or flower? Draw a picture of it below.
Tell why it is your favorite.

What I Hope to See at the Botanic Garden

Draw what you imagine you will see at the botanic garden.

Explore

NAME:

DATE:

LOCATION:

What I Observed at the Botanical Garden

Imagine you are on a plant safari. Draw a plant that you "discovered" at the botanic garden.

What I Observed at the Botanical Garden

Imagine you are on a plant safari. Draw another plant that you "discovered" at the botanic garden.

Expand

Comparing Plants

Look at your two pictures very carefully.

Describe how the two plants are alike.

Describe how the two plants are different.

NAME:

DATE:

LOCATION:

Observing Ecosystems

Many botanical gardens have exhibits that recreate ecosystems from other parts of the world. Imagine you are on a botanical safari.

Draw one ecosystem below.

Describe the climate: amount of sunshine, rain, average temperature, seasonal change. How is this climate different from our climate? In what ways is it the same?

Explore

Observing Ecosystems

Many botanical gardens have exhibits that recreate ecosystems from other parts of the world. Imagine you are on a botanical safari.

Draw another ecosystem below.

Describe the climate: amount of sunshine, rain, average temperature, seasonal change. How is this climate different from our climate? In what ways is it the same?

 **Expand**

Comparing and Contrasting Ecosystems

How are these ecosystems the same?

How are these ecosystems different?

Dichotomous Sorting of Objects or Organisms

Pick a property you observed that only some plants have. Use it to sort the plants you observed into two groups, those with that property and those without. Record your work with words and/or drawings in each column. Select another property and try again.

With Property_____	Without Property_____

Select another property and sort the objects above again below.

With Property _____	Without Property _____	With Property _____	Without Property _____

 **Evaluate**

NAME:

DATE:

LOCATION:

The Most Interesting Things I Learned
What are the most interesting things you learned from your trip to the botanic garden?

City Parks

According to the *Benchmarks for Science Literacy*, urban children should have the opportunity to observe a variety of plants and animals in their neighborhood and at parks.

New York City's urban parks are a natural laboratory for field exploration that is free and open to all visitors 365 days a year. They are natural places to go to observe geological features such as landforms, rocks and soils, ponds, lakes, and streams. Although landscaped and managed for over 100 years, most city parks include natural botanical features, including stands of native deciduous and evergreen trees and understory plants as well as introduced exotic plants, both wild and cultivated. The city parks are an oasis for wildlife, including both native and introduced mammals, insects, and birds. They are natural places to go to observe seasonal changes.

Geology

New York City parks are an excellent place to explore geology. All major New York City parks contain geological features resulting from the Wisconsin Ice Sheet, a glacier that covered most of the area 50,000 years ago. Where did the glacier come from? Fifty thousand years ago, the Earth was in an Ice Age. Constant cold temperatures meant that snow accumulated from year to year and did not melt and flow away as it does today in our temperate climate. North America was buried under a sheet of ice 1,000 feet thick that reached what would become New York from the arctic, spanning from coast to coast. In Canada, the ice sheet was up to 3,000 feet thick. The glacier oozed slowly south under the weight of each year's accumulated snow and ice, dragging along detached bedrock, sediment, clay, and soil from northern lands. It even detached huge boulders from the bedrock and carried them along. In some areas, it scoured away the soil and exposed the underlying bedrock. Wherever the bedrock is exposed, you may be able to see grooves carved into the stone by boulders scraping over their surface as the glacier moved. This is most clearly evident in Manhattan's Central Park.

When the climate began to warm about 30,000 years ago, the rubble-filled ice began to melt from its southernmost edge, dropping boulders, rocks, gravel, sand,

and silt. The glacier continued to ooze southward under its own weight. Boulders trapped rocks and sediment piled slowly higher, ultimately forming long ridges of hills that run through Staten Island, Brooklyn, Queens, and eastern Long Island. This belt of hills is known as a *terminal moraine*. The landscape architects of New York City parks built upon this framework left behind by the glacier.

The terminal moraines contain rocks that formed far away in very different geological conditions than the local bedrock. Glacial boulders left behind on the surface may have formed tens, hundreds, or thousands of miles away. Local bedrock is composed mostly of mica schist and gneiss. The mica schist is dark grey with silvery sparkles of mica. The gneiss (pronounced "nice") is a metamorphic rock with banding. Dark grey rock with a uniform texture might be basalt from the Pallisades in New Jersey. Pink granite may have traveled all the way from the mountains of Maine. Most of the glacial rock is worn smooth and rounded from its travels and tumbles in the icy, rock-filled meltwater of the retreating glacier. Bring a field guide to rocks with you on your trips to New York City parks to help you identify the different rocks you encounter.

The melting glacial waters washed the land to the south with a constant stream. These meltwater-washed lands became flat plains called *outwash plains*; they are found throughout southern Staten Island, Brooklyn, and Queens.

Fields and Forests

Many city parks have large open grassy areas for sports and recreation, these are lawns. True meadows, unlike lawns, are flat areas where grasses and herbaceous plants are allowed to grow, flower, and seed. They provide important habitat for insects, birds, and small mammals.

The major parks highlighted in this book also contain forested areas. The native northeastern forest ecosystem was originally dominated by oak and hickory trees. Oaks still make up a large part of most city park forests, including native red, white, and pin oaks. Other common native trees in city parks include black cherry, sweetgum, tulip, sugar, and red maple. There are also white and green ash and American elm. The forest's understory of shrubs, flowers, and herbaceous plants provides food and shelter for many small animals.

Younger children can explore the forest by collecting fallen leaves and seeds to explore the biodiversity of the forest. (Do not allow children to take seeds or leaves from the living trees.) Which kinds of trees do they find the most? How are the leaves the same and how are they different? Most leaves will be flat to collect a lot of sun, and will have veins. Veins in leaves are like our veins—they carry fluids and nutrients from one part of the body to the other. Veins in leaves bring sugars formed by photosynthesis to the rest of the tree and bring water absorbed by the roots to the leaves. Older children can try their hand at identifying

Science Safaris in New York City

trees using a field guide. You can download a simple tree leaf identification guide from the New York City Department of Parks Project Greenstreets website at www. nycgovparks.org/sub_your_park/trees_greenstreets.html.

City Park Wildlife

Most visitors to New York City parks will be surprised at the wide variety of wild creatures that make their homes in the parks. New York City parks offer wildlife a wide variety of habitats. The food and shelter provided by these habitats support a complex food web. The waters are home to reptiles such as red-eared sliders and painted turtles and to amphibians such as frogs and toads. Crustaceans such as crayfish may be found in the waters of New York City parks, as well as the terrestrial crustaceans known as pillbugs or sowbugs. Fish species may include bluegills, sunfish, and large-mouth bass. Among the mammals you may encounter in city parks are the Eastern chipmunk, white-footed mouse, cottontail rabbit, raccoon, and little brown bat. These shy animals are most likely to be observed at dusk. North America's only marsupial, the possum, may also be spied.

New York City parks are excellent sites for bird watching. The parks are major stopovers for birds migrating along the Atlantic Flyway. Birds feed on a host of insects, from ants and cicadas to wasps and caterpillars; on other invertebrates such as worms, pillbugs, and millipedes; and on the herbs and seeds of the meadows and forests.

Local resident birds are also interesting. Observe the mating behaviors of pigeons, or the nest-building of American robins. Many of our most-familiar local birds were actually exotic introduced species. Pigeons, house sparrows, and starlings were all imported from Europe. Others are notable for their bright colors, such as the bright red northern cardinals and the aptly named bluejays. Bring a field guide to birds to help you identify birds, or stop by the Audubon Center at Prospect Park for expert advice.

Waterfowl feed on the aquatic invertebrates, plants, and fish of the lakes, ponds, and streams. The ducks, swans, and geese that are year-round residents of city lakes and ponds are the easiest birds for young children to observe because they are large, slow–moving, and unafraid of people. You may also see migrating waterfowl or seasonal residents. You may see hybrid ducks formed from natural matings between domestic and wild ducks. Point out adaptations to life in the water such as long legs, webbed feet, and large, flattened bills for straining food from the water. Only the American coots, which look like little black hens, and the gulls lack the webbed feet characteristic of many waterfowl. It is best not to feed the birds, but if you must, please bring only whole-grain, unprocessed food such as unsweetened puffed wheat. Processed foods are unhealthy for wildlife.

Human Impacts

Understanding the impact of human activities on natural systems is an important science concept that is part of the core curriculum in science. All forested urban parks illustrate common human impacts on natural woodlands. Three human impacts threaten the health of park woodlands: non-native invasive species, soil compaction, and soil erosion.

Non-native or exotic species came to the area from Europe and Asia's temperate regions due to human activities. Some came accidentally as seeds in imported cargo; others were imported deliberately by settlers, farmers, botanists; and gardeners. Park designers planted both native and non-native species. Unfortunately, many of these exotic species have been too successful, out-competing native trees. Overly successful non-native trees like the Norway maple and Sycamore maple are interfering with the natural interdependence between indigenous plants and wildlife because they do not provide the food and shelter that native animals obtain from native plants.

Human activity also hurts the forest soil. Healthy forest soil is loose, with many pockets of air and room for water to move through. In a healthy forest, the burrowing of worms and other soil creatures help to keep the soil porous. Forests can handle the traveling of native animals and the occasional human visitor. But city parks are visited by millions of people every year. When too many people walk on the soil, especially when it is wet, the soil is pushed down into these air spaces. The soil becomes hard and dense. There is little room for air and water. Roots cannot penetrate. Seedlings cannot break through the compacted soil and the forest cannot renew itself. Plants begin to die and the soil becomes bare.

Soil erosion is another problem in city parks that results from human activity. Soil erosion is related to soil compaction. Prospect Park is hilly. When the soil on slopes becomes bare due to compaction, there is no vegetation to slow down rainwater. Rushing rainwater carries away the soil. The slopes begin to erode. Signs of erosion include muddy puddles on pathways at the bottom of slopes. You may see what look like little river valleys in the hillside. Roots become exposed. Exposed roots hurt trees, resulting in fallen limbs and peeling bark. New growth cannot take hold to stop the erosion.

Help your child notice the signs of human impact in the park. Younger children will notice litter, or perhaps footprints or bicycle tire tracks in the bare soil. Ask them to look for areas of the park where nothing is growing. Older children may notice the beaten trails that people have created through the woods in addition to the paved paths. For all investigations in the park, the most important things you will need are proper clothing for the weather, sturdy walking shoes, and your powers of observation. To help you plan your visit, you can download maps of the parks from the New York City Department of Parks website. You can also download aerial photos from Google Maps.

Urban Park Rangers Nature Centers

New York City parks include fifteen Urban Park Ranger Nature Centers. Each serves as an in-park community center for public education and environmental studies. The centers offer walking tours and workshop sites for educational programs for classes and families. Nature center exhibits highlight the diversity of the landscape and provide informational material like trail maps, nature center brochures, and *Outdoors in NYC*, the Rangers' quarterly newspaper and calendar.

The Natural Classroom hands-on programs for students are available through New York City's nature centers staffed by Urban Park Rangers. There are nature centers in all five boroughs:

- The Bronx—Crotona Park, Pelham Bay (Orchard Beach), and Van Cortlandt Park.

- Brooklyn—Prospect Park (The Audubon Center), Fort Green Park, and Marine Park (The Saltmarsh Nature Center).

- Manhattan—Central Park (Belvedere Castle and Dana Discovery Center).

- Queens—Alley Pond Park, Forest Park, and Fort Totten Park.

- Staten Island—Blue Heron Nature Center, and Greenbelt Nature Center.

Programs are offered for students in grades K–8. There are activities for every season. With each program, class groups visit a New York City nature center and take part in a series of hands-on activities led by an Urban Park Ranger. In colder months, a ranger can visit the classroom in conjunction with a separate park visit. There are currently ten natural history programs. These programs are designed to help students meet Department of Education performance standards in science, including observation, measurement, data collection, and analysis.

Program topics include New York City Trees; Urban Raptors (eagles, hawks, owls, and others); Citizen Science: Water Quality Testing; Botany (photosynthesis, plant life cycles, urban ecosystems); Park Conservation (vegetation mapping, habitat assessment, rehabilitation of disturbed natural areas); Urban Park Ecology; Entomology (invertebrate life cycles, anatomy, and adaptations); Geology (the diverse geological features of the city); Ichthyology (fish anatomy, aquatic ecology, and fishing techniques); and Ornithology (bird identification and behavior).

Other cultural programs that develop science understanding and skills focus on orienteering and map reading and Native American relationships with the natural environment.

Current fees are $100 per program. Find out about current programs and how to register at the Urban Rangers website. Plan well ahead for your choice of dates. http://www.nycgovparks.org/sub_about/parks_divisions/urban_park_rangers/pd_ur_natural_class.html#natural

National Parks of New York Harbor

The National Parks of New York Harbor administers 23 unique sites in New York and northern New Jersey. It encompasses over 27,000 acres, including a large national recreation area, national monuments, national memorials, and national historic sites.

The Statue of Liberty National Monument and Ellis Island are two of the most famous and well-visited sites. The African Burial Ground, Governors Island National Monument, and Floyd Bennett Field are three other sites that are not only culturally and historically significant, but can offer glimpses into the original geology and natural landscape of New York City.

The Gateway National Recreation Area has a number of places where people can enjoy activities in the outdoors. It has three units—Jamaica Bay, Staten Island, and Sandy Hook—where people can enjoy fishing, swimming, boating, birding, and nature study in designated areas.

Beaches, dunes, salt marshes, freshwater ponds, meadows, and forests are the different ecosystems that one can encounter in the Gateway National Recreation Area. Each unit has ranger-led special events and activities, such as nature walks, bird watching, and conservation events that allow you to learn more about the flora, fauna, and physical settings of the different ecosystems found in the parks. In this book, we highlight several areas of special interest: Jamaica Bay Wildlife Refuge, Great Kills Park, Plum Beach, Fort Tilden, Fort Wadsworth and Dead Horse Bay.

For more information about the National Parks of New York Harbor, check the website: www.nps.gov/npnh/index.htm.

Alley Pond Park

At 657 acres, Alley Pond Park is the second largest park in Queens. Like many city parks, Alley Pond Park was created around naturally occurring glacial features that made the land less attractive for farming and development. This park has natural features not found in many other parks, like its freshwater and saltwater wetlands and tidal flats. Alley Pond Park also has extensive meadows in addition to forested areas. It offers diverse ecosystems and supports abundant wildlife. The close juxtaposition of so many varied habitats makes Alley Pond Park a natural site for environmental education. When the Alley Pond Park Nature Trail opened in 1935, it was the first nature trail in the city's park system.

Glacial Features

Alley Pond Park lies on a glacier-formed moraine. It offers many glacial features to observe. The park is nestled in a classic U-shaped glacial valley, carved by the passing ice. The melting of buried chunks of glacial ice formed the ponds dispersed throughout the valley. Alley Pond Park may offer the best example of these kettle ponds of all the city parks. The boulders scattered on the hillsides of the southern end of the park were deposited by the melting ice of the glacier.

The surrounding glacial hills allow groundwater to drain into the valley. This freshwater bubbles up from natural springs that mix with the saltwater from Little Neck Bay, creating freshwater and saltwater wetlands and tidal flats. In the 1930s, much of the marshland was filled in. Marshland is now recognized as vital to a healthy ecosystem. In 1974, the city began rehabilitating the natural wetlands of the park.

True meadows are flat areas where grasses and herbaceous plants are allowed to grow, flower, and seed. They provide important habitat for insects, birds, and small mammals.

Wetland Wildlife

The park offers wildlife a wide variety of habitats. The food and shelter provided by the park's fresh and brackish waters support complex food webs. The waters are home to fish, reptiles, and amphibians. In spring, listen to the chorus of the spring peepers. Once widespread throughout Long Island, these tiny frogs prefer a woodland environment but depend upon wetlands for their reproduction. Look for their tadpoles in ponds during the spring. Alley Pond Park includes a 23-acre bird sanctuary. The park is a major stopover for birds migrating along the Atlantic Flyway. With its freshwater ponds and streams and saltmarsh and tidal flats, Alley Pond Park attracts the most diverse waterfowl of the city parks. Point out adaptations to life in the water such as long legs, webbed feet, and large, flattened bills for straining food from the water or pointed beaks for spearing fish. As in other city parks, you may encounter Eastern chipmunks, cottontail rabbits, or raccoons.

Blue Heron Park

This Staten Island park is named after the blue heron, a four-foot tall grey wading bird that may be observed standing at the edge of a pond or marsh, watching for fish or frogs. The blue heron can be found in aquatic environments throughout the New York area. The Visitors Center contains classrooms, exhibit areas, a library, restrooms, and observation decks with bird feeders and a mist net

for bird banding. Educational programs are provided by the Urban Park Rangers and the Friends of Blue Heron, a community-based organization.

This 236-acre wetland is one of the city's newest parks (officially dedicated on October 22, 1996), and it not only provides a haven for wildlife and an environmental education resource, it also helps to control the flooding of Staten Island streets. It is part of the Staten Island Bluebelt, a nationally recognized, award-winning innovation in natural storm water management and wetland preservation. New York City once contained 224,000 acres of freshwater wetlands. These valuable ecosystems slow erosion, prevent flooding by retaining storm waters, and filter and decompose pollutants. They are highly productive and diverse ecosystems. Urbanization has resulted in most of the city's wetlands being filled for construction or dredged for transport. Only 1 percent of the city's historic freshwater wetlands remain today.

Urban wetlands are especially valuable for flood control because streets and rooftops cannot absorb rainfall and they increase surface water runoff. Street and residential flooding were common in the developed marshlands of Staten Island. Instead of merely constructing new storm sewers, the New York City Department of Environmental Protection decided to follow nature's water management plan and constructed an engineered wetland that integrates traditional drainage infrastructure with natural wetlands. The multidisciplinary design team involved ecologists, hydrologists, engineers, and wetland scientists. The resulting landscape is beautiful, serene, and supports a thriving wetland habitat. The Bluebelt program saved tens of millions of dollars in infrastructure costs when compared to constructing conventional storm sewers.

Blue Heron Park contains over 200 acres of meadows, ponds, streams, and woodlands. The park also holds six kettle ponds formed by the Wisconsin glacier. The largest pond in the park, Spring Pond, is a dead tree swamp with stumps protruding from the water. Other ponds teem with life. White water lilies provide cover for breeding tree frogs and spring peepers. Turtles sun on logs. Raccoons forage along the water's edge. Birds such as the glossy ibis, the black-crowned night heron, belted kingfishers, wood ducks, owls, and osprey are year-round residents. In addition to housing these natives, the park provides resting and feeding grounds for migrating birds as they travel along the Atlantic flyway.

Before your trip, watch a video about the Bluebelt at http://www.nyc.gov/html/dep/html/dep_projects/bluebelt_video.shtml.

Central Park

Central Park occupies 840 acres in the bustling center of Manhattan. The park is considered one of the world's greatest achievements in urban landscaping. Planned by Frederick Law Olmstead and Calvert Vaux, it was designed to both "preserve and enhance" the natural features of the terrain. Central Park is often referred to as the heart and lungs of Manhattan.

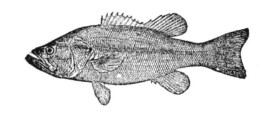

With more than 24,000 trees, the park provides the opportunity to observe urban forests, meadows, and seven artificial lakes and ponds. A recent survey conducted by the New York State Department of Environmental Conservation (DEC) found that the lakes are home to at least nine different species of freshwater fish: largemouth bass, black crappie, yellow perch, bluegill, pumpkinseed, carp, brown bullhead, golden shiner, and common shiner. The Charles A. Dana Discovery Center, located at the northeast corner of the Harlem Meer at 110th Street between Fifth and Lenox Avenues, loans fishing gear for catch-and-release fishing in the Meer from April through October.

One of the best ponds for nature observations is Turtle Pond, located near Belvedere Castle. It was named in 1987 in honor of its most prominent residents. This pond began as a shallow pool that attracted fish, frogs, turtles, dragonflies, and aquatic fowl. Today it is a tiny constructed ecosystem. In 1997, the shoreline was redesigned to meet the needs of the many animals—aquatic, amphibian, reptilian, and avian—that call it home. A variety of plants were planted around the shoreline, concealing the concrete edges of the pond. A new island—Turtle Island—was added to the pond to provide a spot for turtles to build their nests. There are sandy spots for the turtles to lay their eggs. The turtles can be observed from many great spots along the shoreline as well as from Belvedere Castle.

But Central Park is perhaps most notable for its geological features. The park is a popular site for college geology field trips. Outcrops of the underlying bedrock provide the opportunity to observe the hidden support of the Manhattan skyline. The glacial terrain typical of the outer boroughs will not support the construction of tall buildings as does the bedrock in Manhattan. Exposures of the Manhattan schist bedrock emerge throughout the park, particularly in its southern end. Manhattan schist is a medium gray, layered metamorphic rock, sprinkled throughout with sparkles of shiny, thin mica. You may also see Fordham gneiss (pronounced "nice"), with an almost striped, often wavy look. The pressures of continents in collision created the Manhattan schist and Fordham gneiss outcrops enjoyed by sunbathers and students of geology alike. The Manhattan bedrock is all that remains of an ancient mountain chain worn down by the forces of erosion acting over millions of years.

Although millions of feet travel over the exposed bedrock, the shiny surfaces are glacially-polished. Striations and grooves can be observed that were carved by rocks embedded in the base of the Wisconsin ice sheet as it moved southward. Umpire Rock, near 63rd Street and Central Park West, provides an especially good example of glacial grooves. Glacial erratic boulders of local and more distant origins can be found scattered around the park, particularly on the exposed bedrock and around the park ponds. Local schist and gneiss has also been used to build garden walls and bridges within the park, although much of the construction stone may have been transported to the park.

Outcrops and boulders of gneiss show evidence of the varying weathering rates of different minerals. The quartz-rich layers tend to resist weathering. They stand out and maintain their glacial polish, while faster-weathering bands of feldspar and mica weather away to create recessed surfaces.

Central Park is also home to New York's main weather station. Temperature, precipitation, and snowfall for New York are all measured in Central Park. The station is located at Belvedere Castle, atop the second highest natural elevation in the park. A state-of-the-art meteorological data station is located just below the Castle. The Castle provides a panoramic view in almost every direction from its tower. Designed in 1865 as a Victorian "Folly," the castle holds a collection of natural history artifacts (skeletons, paper mache birds) as well as microscopes and telescopes, all designed to give young visitors an insight into the methodology of natural science. Visitors can borrow field packs that contain binoculars, reference material, maps, and notepaper, which can all be used to explore the park. The Castle is also a great place to watch for the park's resident birds of prey, including hawks, kestrels, and osprey. Check for special programs for the public offered by the Central Park Conservancy and the Urban Park Rangers.

Central Park visit planning notes:

Clove Lakes Park

Located in Staten Island, Clove Lakes Park is one of the city's Forever Wild Preserves. It covers slightly over 130 acres and has forest, meadows, salt marsh, and freshwater wetlands habitats. The name Clove comes from the Dutch word "kloven," which means *cleft* and refers to the valley between two hills—Emerson and Grymes—that form this park. This valley was formed by the Wisconsin glacier and originally had a brook running through it. (It is U-shaped like a classic glacial valley rather than V-shaped like a river valley.) However, this brook was dammed and several lakes formed in the region over the years, including the ones that you encounter in the park. The park has a famous tulip tree; at over 100 feet tall, it is the largest living thing on Staten Island. The tree is at least 300 years old. What other kinds of plants and trees do you encounter in this park? Use your tree guide to help.

Unique features of this park are the green-gray serpentinite rock outcroppings. This exposed rock is a part of the serpentinite ridge that runs through Staten Island and is exposed in some of the upland areas. You will notice that there are not many trees and plants growing in this rock. This is because the trees cannot tolerate the high concentrations of magnesium that make up this metamorphic rock. It is an example of a highly restricted and stressed ecosystem that isn't because of human impacts. This is the same rock that forms Todt Hill, which at 410 feet above sea level is the highest elevation point on the Eastern Seaboard south of Maine. Interestingly, the name Todt comes from a Dutch word meaning "dead." Some geologists believe it was so named because of the lack of trees and plants in the exposed rocks.

Forest Park

Forest Park is aptly named. It is one of the last natural densely forested parks in New York City, containing the largest continuous oak forest in Queens. Of the park's 538 acres, 413 are heavily forested with native northern red, scarlet and white oak. Some of these trees are over 150 years old. Other natives trees include the tuliptree, shagbark hickory, and wild black cherry. The under-story includes dogwood, sassafras, and corktree.

Forest Park has one of the largest pine groves in the parks of New York City. White pine forests originally covered much of northeastern North America, but unlike the park's deciduous forest, the pine grove in Forest Park is not a naturally occurring forest. The pine grove was first planted in 1914, with 2,500 trees. For the park's centennial celebration in 1995, 100 new trees were planted. Three nature trails meander through the forest, gully, and pine grove. This wooded area can also be explored on horseback.

Like Prospect Park, Forest Park was conceived before the consolidation of the five boroughs into present-day New York City. Frederick Law Olmsted surveyed the park and designed the Forest Park Drive.

Glacial Geology

The high hills of Forest Park are part of the Harbor Hill terminal moraine of Long Island, molded by the Wisconsin glacier. The park topography is glacial "knob and kettle terrain," with the characteristic irregular surface of hillocks and scattered kettles. Kettles are depressions in glacial outwash formed by the melting of a detached mass of glacial ice. Urban Park Rangers offer periodic introductions to Forest Park's geology.

Forest Park rests between the North and South shores of Long Island at one of its narrowest points. The high hills of Forest Park offer views of Long Island Sound to the north and the Atlantic Ocean to the south, providing children with the opportunity to imagine that Long Island really is a landform that is surrounded by water. Long Island is the largest island in the continental United States. Preceed or follow you trip by looking at aerial photos of Forest Park. Use Google Maps to help you visualize the terrain.

Wildlife

The extensive woodlands of Forest Park offer wildlife a haven and support a complex food web. Among the mammals commonly found in the park are the

Eastern chipmunk, white-footed mouse, cottontail rabbit, and raccoon. Quail are among the unusual forest residents to be found in Forest Park. Quail are small, plump birds in the pheasant family that spend their lives on the forest floor. They are predominantly seed eaters but will also eat insects, worms, and similar critters. They nest on the ground and are capable of only short, rapid bursts of flight. The park is a major stopover for birds migrating along the Atlantic Flyway and offers excellent bird watching.

Forest Park visit planning notes:

Great Kills Park

Great Kills Park is a part of the Gateway National Recreation Area. It spans 580 acres and includes nature trails and a beach. The park is a great place for bird watching. Great Kills Park has the only osprey nesting site on Staten Island. The Lenape people who originally inhabited the region took advantage of the rich oyster beds and the many herbaceous plants found here for food and medicine. Today, Great Kills provides a wonderful opportunity to observe the wild animal and plant life in different ecosystems.

History of Trash

Walking along the park's wooded paths, you may come across pieces of broken china and pottery buried in the soil. These pieces emerge from the incinerated materials that were used to create the park. In the 1940s, when much of New York City's trash was burned, an incinerator was built near the site, which would become Great Kills Park. Tons of ash and cinder, including the materials that did not incinerate, were carted to the site and covered with sand and organic waste from sewage treatment plants. Over the years, this mixture decomposed and became the soil that now nourishes the plants and trees that you see in the park.

In addition to forests, Great Kills Park has beaches, sand dunes, and a salt marsh to explore, along with a small, artificial freshwater pond. The Educational Field Station/Discovery Center is a great place to start your exploration. There you will find information about the park and a park ranger to answer any questions that you might have. The Discovery Center is adjacent to the pond; spend some time there and notice how many different plants and insects you can find. You might want to bring mosquito repellant; although mosquitoes are annoying to us, they are an essential source of food for birds, fish, amphibians, and other insects that live in or around the pond.

Pioneer Forest

The Nature Trail will lead you through a characteristic pioneer forest. In addition to newly planted pine trees and hosts of annual and perennial plants, you will also find deciduous trees like the ailanthus and black cherry. These trees are pioneer plants since they are usually the first to inhabit a place with nutrient-poor soil. They thrive in these conditions and make way for other plants, like oaks, to later take root.

The beach has characteristic dunes that protect the forest from beach erosion. You will see dune grass and may get a glimpse of the rare sandwort. With rhizomatous (interconnected) roots, these plants hold the sand in place. Be careful not to walk on the sand dunes, because although these plants are doing a tough job, they are quite delicate and our feet could kill them. Explore the beach for evidence of the kinds of animals that live there. What do you see? You may encounter the shells of oysters, clams, moon snails, and horseshoe crabs. Use your seashore field guide to help you identify what you find.

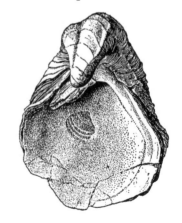

At Great Kills Park you can explore the beach and forest in the same day. You could notice how the plants change as you move from the sand dunes to the forest. For more information about the history of the park and the animals and plants that live there, pick up "Family Field Guide to the Natural Areas of Great Kills Park" at the Discovery Center. In addition to your collection of field guides, it will be a great companion to your excursion.

 *Great Kills Park visit planning notes:*

Marine Park

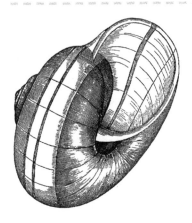

Marine Park is one of Brooklyn's best-kept secrets. Many locals are familiar with the park for its baseball and cricket fields; however, at over 520 acres, Marine Park is Brooklyn's largest park and also a Forever Wildlife Preserve. The park surrounds Gerritsen Creek, the westernmost freshwater inlet of the Jamaica Bay area. The bay is the result of over 5,000 years of accumulated sand deposited by ocean currents. The sand formed the barrier islands that protect the bay from the strong ocean currents and allowed salt marshes to grow. These salt marshes are important reproduction and feeding sites for birds, bony fish, mollusks, and crustaceans. The barrier islands that protect Marine Park and Jamaica

Bay are the Rockaways. In addition to the salt marshes, Marine Park has sand dunes and meadows; it is a great place to observe and study different coastal ecosystems. Gerritsen Creek supplies freshwater to Marine Park. This enables the area to support a wider diversity of living things than if it only had ocean water.

Marine Park is a favorite among birdwatchers (over 300 species of birds live in the area!). Because it has a sheltered creek and wetlands, it attracts a wide variety of waterfowl including duck, geese, cormorants, herons, egrets, and sandpipers. It is also one of the city's nesting sites for the osprey, an elegant raptor. The osprey eats almost exclusively fish, which makes Marine Park and other coastal marshes prime habitat for this bird. Like owls, the outer toes of the osprey are reversible. This makes it easy for them to catch slippery fish! They like to build their nests in tall places like in the forks of dead trees and utility poles. In several of our local parks, specially designed nesting platforms have been built to ensure that the ospreys have adequate nesting sites. See if you can spot one in Marine Park. You can also look for them in Pelham Bay, Great Kills, and Jamaica Bay.

Birds are attracted to Marine Park because it has a great density and variety of flora, ranging from marsh grasses and sedges to low-lying shrubs and woody trees. Sedges may look like grasses, but they are different because many of them have triangle stems and they are often associated with wetlands. You will also find poke-weed, primrose, bayberry, and blackberry plants, which provide food and shelter for wetland animals. Many of these plants are also used as traditional medicine and food by different human cultures. Naturalists in Marine Park have learned that even the invasive phragmites play an important role in purifying the air and soil as well as providing food and shelter for animals, especially once all other sources are depleted. You will notice that many phragmites reeds maintain their feathery heads during much of the winter. Many birds and land animals have developed a taste for these seeds. This is another example of adaptation, in this case of native species adapting to the presence of an exotic species and learning to use it as a resource.

To learn more about salt marshes and Marine Park, visit the Salt Marsh Nature Center. It is located in the park on Ave. U and Burnett St. and is easily accessible by public transportation. The center offers educational programs for schools and the talks, arts and crafts, and nature walks for families. Teachers can call 1-866-NYC-HAWK for more information about specialized educational programs. Families should visit the Salt Marsh Alliance website (www.saltmarshalliance.org) for an up-to-date calendar of events.

Marine Park visit planning notes:

Prospect Park

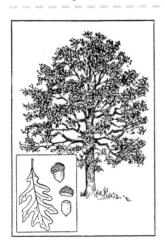

Prospect Park is a natural oasis in the heart of Brooklyn for people and wildlife. The park was designed and constructed in the 1860s by the great landscape architects Frederick Law Olmsted and Calvert Vaux, whose parks are noted for incorporating natural features. Prospect Park spans 585 acres. Its large size and rugged and varied terrain make a day in the park almost like a trip to the Adirondacks. The park is an excellent place to explore both geology and ecology. You can explore meadows, forests, lakes, ponds, and streams. Download a map of Prospect Park (http://www.prospectpark.org/) to orient yourself before exploring.

Geology

Before exploring the geology of the park, it is important to understand that—like most New York City parks—Prospect Park has a glacier known as the Wisconsin Ice Sheet to thank for its basic structure. The glacial features of Prospect Park are common throughout the undeveloped landscapes of the northern United States. These glacial features include hills, meadows, kettle ponds, and outwash plains, all of which can be found in Prospect Park. As you explore Prospect Park, younger children can see and explore ponds and streams, meadows, and hills to develop a concrete understanding of the basic types of landforms. Older children can think about how the power of water and ice created the landscape.

The northern edge of Prospect Park is formed from glacial till, composed of rocks of all sizes, ranging from huge boulders to sand and silt in a random mix that is characteristic of lands formed from glacial debris. You can see a moles-eye-view cross section through glacial till in the New York State Environment exhibit at the American Museum of Natural History. You can imagine the boulders lying buried in the hills of Prospect Park by observing the large boulders scattered around the park and those used to build the walls in the Ravine. Where did all of these rocks come from? They came from the north, from New Jersey, upstate New York, and Canada. Explore the surface of the large boulders and notice how smooth and rounded they are. This polish is the result of being tumbled in the rock- and sand-filled glacial meltwaters, like in a huge rock tumbler.

The terrain of Prospect Park slopes continually downward from the northern glacial highlands to the southern outwash plain, composed of flat sandy land. This slope is punctuated by a ridge of hills that are part of the terminal moraine. The southern edge of the park lies on sand and gravel left behind by the melting glacier. Prospect Park's 60-acre Lake was dug from this flat, open terrain of the outwash plain.

To create the Ravine, Prospect Park's landscape designers drew inspiration from the mountain streams and pools of the Adirondack Mountains. They joined natural glacial kettle ponds formed from large chunks of the retreating glacial ice to create the park's man-made watercourse. While the hills of the park were formed by nature, the gorge through the Ravine, with its winding streams and waters leading into the Lake, was created from the imagination of the landscape architects. The 60-acre Lake is was excavated as part of the construction of the park and is the only freshwater lake in Brooklyn. It is fed by both rain and by New York City tap water.

Forest and Fields

Prospect Park contains the last remaining indigenous eastern deciduous forest in Brooklyn. Almost half of the park, 250 acres, is forested. The native forest ecosystem was originally dominated by oak and hickory trees. Oaks still make up a large part of the park's forest, including native red, white, and pin oaks. The age of a tree that has fallen can be calculated by counting the yearly growth rings in the trunk. A black oak that fell during a storm was found to be 220 years old. Finding out the age of a living tree is an invasive process that can damage the tree, so we don't know the exact age of most living trees in the park, but many are likely to be at least as old. Other common native trees in the park include black cherry, sweetgum, tulip, sugar maple, and red maple. There are also white and green ash and American elm. A small stand of white pines can be found at the northern end of the Long Meadow. There are over 150 species of trees in Prospect Park, including native and exotic species.

The forest's understory of shrubs, flowers, and herbaceous plants provides food and shelter for many small animals.

True meadows are flat areas where grasses and herbaceous plants are allowed to grow, flower, and seed. They provide important habitat for insects, birds, and small mammals. There are two "true" meadows in the Park: one by the Upper Pool in the Ravine and one on Lookout Hill.

Wildlife

Prospect Park offers wildlife a variety of habitats. The food and shelter provided by the park's waters support a complex food web. The waters are home to reptiles such as red-eared sliders and painted turtles. Amphibians such as frogs breed in the waters, as do crayfish, freshwater cousins of lobsters in the crustacean family. Fish species include bluegills, sunfish, and large-mouth bass. Migrating and resident birds don't seem to care that the watercourse and lakes are artificial. Among the mammals commonly found in the park are the Eastern chipmunk, white-footed mouse, cottontail rabbit, raccoon, and little brown bat. North America's only marsupial, the possum, is also a park resident.

Around 200 species of birds are permanent or temporary residents of Prospect Park. The park is a major stopover for birds migrating along the Atlantic Flyway. Birds feed on a host of insects, worms, pillbugs, and millipedes and on the herbs and seeds of the meadows and forests. Waterfowl feed on the aquatic invertebrates, plants, and fish of the lakes, ponds, and streams. Ducks, swans, and geese are year-round residents of the lake. You may also see migrating waterfowl or seasonal residents.

Prospect Park visit planning notes:

Pelham Bay Park

Located in the northeastern corner of the Bronx, Pelham Bay Park is the largest of New York City's parks. With over 2,700 acres, it is three times as big as Manhattan! The park's mature oak forest, meadows, salt marsh, and tidal habitats provides many different ecosystems to explore, including over 13 miles of shoreline. It has two Forever Wildlife Preserves—Thomas Pell Wildlife Refuge and Hunter Island Marine Sanctuary.

The Hunter Island Marine Sanctuary is one of the best places in New York State to view a marine rocky inter-tidal habitat and tidal pool organisms. Glacial erratics and rocky till characterize this region of the park. The creatures in this habitat are adapted to high-energy ocean wave action. The rocky shore is covered with attached mollusks and algae. These organisms are adapted to live in a constantly changing environment. During a high tide, much of the area is covered in water; during low tide, however, rocks are exposed and many organisms become trapped in small pockets of water called *tidal pools* until the next high tide. There these organisms are in danger of overheating or drying out. Organisms that are commonly found in this habitat include green seaweed, Irish moss, red algae, blue mussels, Northern rock barnacles, and hermit crabs. You may even spot a Forbe's sea star. What are some adaptations that enable creatures to survive in this habitat?

Salt marshes and mud flats are two other important marine ecosystems found in Pelham Bay Park. Salt marshes are important habitats for birds and other animals. Salt marshes play a key role in removing toxins and pollutants from surrounding water, soil, and air. In Pelham, you will notice three different yet distinct salt marsh zones. The high marsh is formed over time by the accumulation of sediments. Daily tides can no longer reach the higher marsh land. The high marsh is flooded only a couple of times every month or during heavy storms. It has marsh grasses and plants that are adapted to live in soil with high salinity.

The inter-tidal marsh and mud flats are regularly inundated with seawater and flooded at least twice a day. The mud flats are formed from sediment from the marsh. Although they appear barren, they are teeming with snails, worms, and burrowing crustaceans. Wading birds frequent the mud flats to feast on the invertebrates that live there.

The Kasimiroff Nature Trail, which begins at the Nature Center on Twin Island, will lead you through the largest oak forest in the park. With white oaks, black oaks, and red oaks, it is a good example of a climax forest in our region. Collect some acorns to see if you can notice the difference between those coming from each variety of oak. Use your tree guide to help and be sure to return the acorns once you are done. You will also find black cherry, Norway spruce, and tulip trees. Hunter Island is a great example of succession. Ranging from sun-loving grasses and wildflowers in the meadows to the tall climax oaks, you will see how plants replace each one another in an ecosystem.

The Thomas Pell Wildlife Sanctuary flanks the Hutchinson River and is home to the Goose Creek and Hutchinson salt marshes and climax oak-hickory forests. Wildlife such as raccoons, hawks, and coyotes inhabit this sanctuary. More than 400 species of animals—birds, fish, mammals, amphibians, reptiles, and insects—have been seen in the park. Follow the Split Rock trail to explore the sanctuary. Compare and contrast the different ecosystems that you see. You might even want to document your observations with a digital camera so that you can learn more about each ecosystem when you return home or to your classroom.

Pelham Bay Park is a green gem in the Bronx. It has great diversity of plants and animals. More than 400 species of birds, fish, mammals, insects, reptiles, amphibians, and invertebrates have been spotted here. How many will you see on your visit? Be sure to bring your tree, bird, and wildlife guides. The park is a great site to visit year-round. It is accessible by public transportation. Visit the New York City Department of Parks and Recreation website (http://www.nycgovparks.org/) for directions, maps, and more information about the park.

Pelham Bay Park visit planning notes:

Fort Tryon Park

Fort Tryon Park is a city, state, and national landmarked park, designed by Frederick Law Olmsted, Jr., son of the architect of Central Park. The park's 67 acres were landscaped for John D. Rockefeller, Jr., who later gifted the park to the City of New York. The park, located at Riverside Drive to Broadway from West 192nd Street to Dyckman Street, is the home of the Cloisters, part of the Metropolitan Museum of Art.

As a science expedition, Fort Tryon Park offers unique geological features. Perhaps the most vertical of the city parks, its narrow, rugged trails and steep stairways hint at the mountains that once rose from this site. One of the highest points in Manhattan, Fort Tryon Park towers above the Hudson River, offering magnificent views of the Palisades and the lower Hudson Valley. To the south and east you can see the Harlem River, the Bronx, and the moraine of the south shore of Long Island Sound as a dark hill along the southern horizon.

Don't miss the opportunity to observe the Palisades across the river. These magnificent cliffs rise to more than 600 feet above the Hudson River's western shore. The Palisades have been designated a "National Natural Landmark." They are considered "the best example of a thick diabase sill in the United States." The Palisades were formed by intrusion of magma (molten rock) between existing layers of rock 192 to 186 million years ago during the late Early Jurassic when dinosaurs walked the Earth. The overlying layers later eroded away, leaving the Palisades at the surface.

The Native Americans called the Hudson River "Muhheakantuck," or "river that flows both ways." Try to see if you can catch the river in the act. See if you can notice objects drifting in the river. Are they heading north or south? (North will be toward your right.) Check again later. Has the river changed its direction? You may even catch it at slack-water, when it is changing direction and for a while it seems to stand still. This occurs because the Hudson River is actually a tidal estuary; at high tide, ocean water pushes into the Hudson, overcoming the river's gentle flow from its headwaters.

Around the base of the Cloisters and along the trail between Fort Tryon and the museum are small exposures of mica schist with bands of gneiss. Outcrops on the west side of the Cloisters along its foundation have excellent examples of glacial striations and grooves.

The Inwood Astronomy Project offers public astronomy programs from Fort Tryon Park. On the second Wednesday of the month (weather permitting), Fort Tryon Park Trust and Jason Kendall of the Inwood Astronomy Project will offer free star and planet gazing in Fort Tryon Park. Telescopes will be available for your use, or bring your own. For more information and weather updates, visit the

Inwood Astronomy Project website (http://www.moonbeam.net/Inwood Astronomy/). Less than half a mile from Inwood Hill Park, try to take a peek at both if you have the energy!

Van Cortlandt Park

Although Van Cortlandt Park is a favorite amongst cross-country runners, many do not know that almost half of the park is also a nature preserve. The park, located in the northern Bronx, contains over 1,100 acres of greenspace. Named after Stephen Van Cortlandt, the first native-born mayor of New York City, the park hosts many historical and natural features that make it a worthwhile trip to learn about the natural and cultural history of New York City. There are several trails that will allow you to explore the park's ancient, diverse terrain. Be sure to bring your tree and plant guides because you may encounter some flora that are rare in our area, such as the sugar maple tree and golden seal herbaceous plant.

Characteristic Forests

With high rocky ridges and low moist valleys, Van Cortlandt Park has a characteristic post-glacial landscape. The two forests, Northwest and Northeast, allow you to observe the differences between the types of flora that grow in different landscapes.

Ask any cross-country runner in New York City about the "back hills." It is a 1.3-mile running trail that leads you through the Northwest Forest—a rocky ridge with exposed bedrock that offers conditioned runners a welcome challenge. Running fast, they may not have time to notice that they are whizzing through an oak-hickory forest, with many century-old trees. With its well-drained soils, the rocky ridge is perfect for this kind of forest. Contrast this with the low, moist Northeast Forest. What kinds of trees are growing there? Look for maples, pin oaks, and tulip trees. Use your tree guide to help!

Can you notice the different layers of the forest? Look up and you will see the tall canopy trees. With their dense leaves, it can get quite shady in the summer. Plants need sunlight to make nutrients and grow through a process called *photosynthesis*. Since these canopy leaves absorb most of the sun's light, how do you think the plants that live in the lower layers have adapted to thrive in this environment? The plants that live in the understory, shrub layer, and ground layer have evolved leaf structures that enable them to survive in shady places. In addition, many of their leaves emerge in the early spring before the tree leaves, enabling them to grow quickly and store the energy to reproduce. These understory shrubs, wildflowers, and grasses provide food and shelter for some of the small birds and mammals that live in Van Cortlandt Park, such as raccoons, foxes, and opossums.

Water Relics

The Old Croton Aqueduct Trail bisects the park. It is a relic of an aqueduct that supplied New York City with water until 1897. The trail runs for about 26 miles into Westchester. In addition to tulip, oak, and maple trees, within the park you can see remnants of the aqueduct's underground tunnel and an old railroad line along the trail.

Van Cortlandt Park is also home to a small freshwater wetland. Fed by Tibbetts Brook (called "Moshulu" by the Lenape people who originally occupied the region), this swamp is an important ecosystem and home to a host of water-loving plants and animals. You will find water lilies and arrowroot in the water and dense stands of cat-tail in the wet soils. Mallards and wood ducks nest there. Herons and egrets visit the wetland to hunt for small fish and frogs. The shy muskrats and nocturnal raccoons also hunt for fish here. See if you can spot any evidence that they were around.

Van Cortlandt Park is a great place to visit year-round to observe animal and plant life in an urban forest. Its diverse landscape allows you to compare and contrast different ecosystems and the flora and fauna that live there. For more information about the different historical sites and extensive facts about the geology of the park, visit the Van Cortlandt pages on the Parks Department website (http://www.nycgovparks.org/parks/VanCortlandtPark/highlights).

Inwood Hill Park

Inwood Hill Park is located at Dyckman Street and the Hudson River, at the Harlem River Ship Canal near the Spuyten Duyvil Creek. The park is famous in New York City history as the place where Native Americans from the Bronx "sold" Manhattan to the Dutch. This historic site is marked by a rock and a plaque. The park has unique geological features and contains the last natural forest and salt marsh in Manhattan.

Geological features include outcrops of Manhattan schist and gneiss. Some outcrops contain garnet crystals. The Wisconsin glacier carved dramatic caves, valleys, and ridges in the terrain. Artifacts have been found in these caves, suggesting their use for shelter by Native Americans. Across the street, in the pocket park on Isham Street and Seaman Avenue, is an outcrop of Inwood marble. This soft stone was quarried by early European settlers for building stone and gravestones. It is found throughout the Bronx and underlies the Hudson River. The park boasts the largest glacial pothole in New York City. Glacial potholes are deep curved holes carved in solid stone steambeds by the scouring action of trapped glacial boulders swirling in rapidly running glacial streams. At least three freshwater springs arise in the park.

The Inwood Hill marsh is all that remains of the extensive salt marshes that once surrounded Manhattan Island. Resident waterfowl found in the marsh include Canada geese, mallard ducks, and ring-billed gulls. Cormorants, great blue herons, great and snowy egrets, and belted kingfishers migrate through or spend the summer.

The majority of the park is a thick deciduous forest, with hiking and nature trails winding up the hill. The forest contains mature red oak and some of the largest native tulip trees in the city. The dry slopes of the hills support a diversity of trees and forest understory. There is also a moist valley between two rock ridges called The Clove, which is covered with wildflowers during the early spring. The forest is home to a wide variety of birds, including hairy woodpeckers and black-capped chickadees. Red-tailed hawks and owls breed in the park. Inwood Hill Park is the site of a bold attempt to reintroduce the Bald Eagle to New York City. Local mammals include raccoons and skunks.

The Nature Center offers information. Urban Park Rangers work with school children to restore the park. Every Saturday (weather permitting), Northern Manhattan Parks and the Inwood Astronomy Project offers free star and planet gazing for the whole family. Telescopes are available or bring your own. For more information, visit the Inwood Astronomy Project website (http://www.moonbeam.net/InwoodAstronomy/).

The riverbank at the north end of the park is a favorite site for fishing. Inwood Hill Park contains one of the city's first kayak/canoe launch sites. A permit is required to operate a kayak or canoe in Parks waterways.

Engage

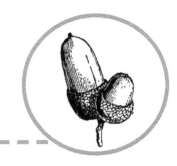

NAME:

DATE:

LOCATION:

My Forest Ecosystem Drawing

Draw a picture of a forest that you have visited before.
Try to remember what you found there.
Use words and/or pictures to show what you expect to find at the forest.

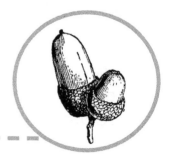

○ **Explore**

NAME:

DATE:

LOCATION:

My Forest Ecosystem Drawing

Visit a forest. Observe it carefully.
Use pictures to show what you found at the forest.

Note: Return any living things to the place where you found them. If you are exploring in a National Park, you should return all objects so that others can also appreciate them.

Explain

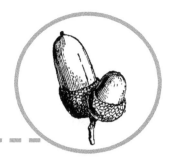

NAME:

DATE:

LOCATION:

My Forest Ecosystem Field Journal Notes

Visit a forest. Observe it carefully.
Use words to describe what you found at the forest.
How do these things interact?

Note: Return any living things to the place where you found them. If you are exploring in a National Park, you should return all objects so that others can also appreciate them.

Expand

Alike and Different: Comparing Living and Nonliving Things

Explore the forest and collect any interesting objects you find. Draw and describe them below.

Living things	Nonliving things

⊸ **Evaluate**

My Forest Ecosystem Human Impacts

Visit a forest. Observe it carefully.
Use words to describe ways that humans have changed this forest ecosystem.
Use words to describe ways that humans have hurt this forest ecosystem.
Use words to describe ways that humans can help this forest ecosystem.

○ **Explore**

Observing carefully is the first step to any scientific investigation. Go to a large city park. Pick an area to observe carefully. Draw and write about the landforms that you see, including hills and meadows, rock formations, streams, ponds, or lakes.

Biodiversity in City Parks

Walk in the park and tally the common park animals that you see.

(**Hint:** Be *quiet* and *move slowly* to see more animal activity.)

Mammals	Birds
Mammals have fur. Female mammals nurse their young. Common mammals in city parks include squirrels, raccoons, chipmunks, opossums, rats, mice, and bats.	*Birds* have feathers. Males and females often both feed their young. Common birds in city parks include pigeons, sparrows, cardinals, starlings, mockingbirds, robins, crows, and hawks.
Draw a picture of any mammals you see on your visit to the park.	Draw a picture of any birds you see on your visit to the park.
How many kinds of mammals did you see on your visit?	How many kinds of birds did you see on your visit?
Which do you think are more diverse in city parks—birds or mammals?	

Biodiversity in City Parks	
Check your park map and see if there is a lake or pond. If so, you may be able to observe some waterfowl. (**Hint:** Be *quiet* and *move slowly* to see more animal activity. If you want to see waterfowl up close, bring some unsweetened puffed wheat or other unsweetened whole grain bread or cereal to scatter. *Do not* hand-feed wild animals. Refined breads and cereals are unhealthy for wild animals.)	
Waterfowl	**Perching and walking birds**
Waterfowl are birds adapted to live near freshwater or saltwater. Common waterfowl in NYC parks include swans, geese, ducks, and coots.	*Perching birds* are adapted to eat, sleep, and nest in trees and bushes. Common perching birds in NYC parks include sparrows, pigeons, and starlings.
Draw a picture of one or more waterfowl, paying special attention to adaptations to life in the water such as webbed feet for swimming and flat beaks for grazing underwater.	**Draw a picture** of one or more perching birds, paying special attention to adaptations to life in trees such as feet for grabbing and pointed beaks for eating seeds and insects.

Expand

NAME:

DATE:

LOCATION:

New York City Park Food Stars

Starting with the primary consumers shown, use observation and inference to figure out what these common park animals eat and what eats them? Put your information together to create a food *star*. If your food stars has connections between the two columns, you can create a food *web*.

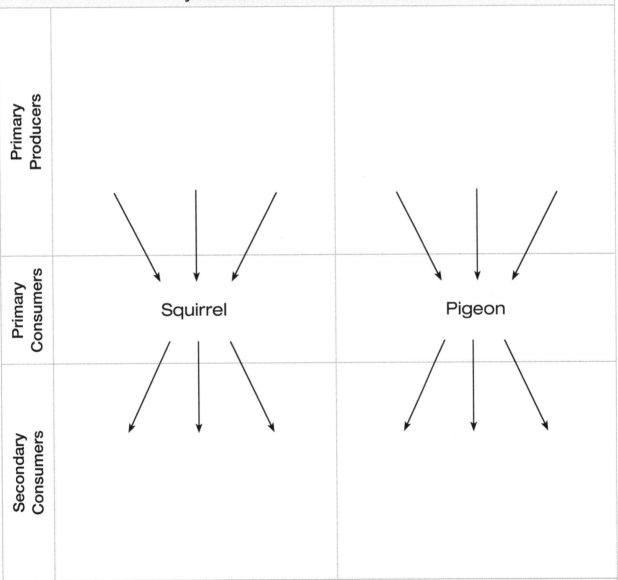

Primary Producers		
Primary Consumers	Squirrel	Pigeon
Secondary Consumers		

Other common residents of New York City parks include the following predators (secondary consumers), hawks, owls, snakes, raccoons, crows, feral cats, and dogs.

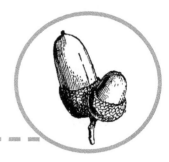

Dichotomous Sorting of Plants or Animals

Pick a property you observed that only *some* living things have. Use it to sort the living things you observed into two groups, those with that property and those without. Record your work with words and/or drawings in each column. Select another property and try again.

With Property _____.	Without Property _____.

Select another property and sort the objects above again in the two columns below.

With Property _____	Without Property _____	With Property _____	Without Property _____

Exotic Introduced Species

What is an exotic introduced species? Any species of animal or plant that is not native to the local ecosystem is considered by ecologists to be exotic—even if it seems very common or ordinary. New York City is home to many exotic introduced species, including some of its most common and familiar plants and animals. Exotic introduced species are found in fields, forests, fresh and salt water, and salt marsh areas. Most exotic introduced species were deliberately or accidentally introduced by the actions of people. It has been estimated that exotic species constitute more than 10 percent of the species in many ecosystems. They are important examples of the impact of human actions on the environment. They are also excellent lenses for gaining understanding of environments and adaptations. According to the World Resources Institute, invasions by non-native species has become such a widespread and critical threat to natural ecosystems that only habitat loss is a greater threat to biodiversity.

Exotic Birds Spread Far and Wide

The three most-common city birds are the pigeon, starling, and house sparrow. Not one of these birds is native to North America. The pigeon was domesticated over a thousand years ago, first as a food source (young birds are eaten as squab) and later for carrying messages. Before their arrival in the New World, these birds were found throughout Europe, the Mediterranean, and in parts of southwest Asia and North Africa. The pigeon was originally brought by settlers to Nova Scotia in the 1600s. The starling and the house sparrow were deliberately introduced into New York City in the 1800s. The house sparrow was introduced in Brooklyn and Central Park and the starling in Central Park. Some additional introductions occurred in other cities. These foreign birds are now found throughout most of the continental United States.

Why did these birds become so common? Each of these species is very adaptable. They are tolerant of a wide ecological range and eat a wide variety of food sources including insects and other invertebrates, fruits and berries, grain, and animal feed. Farms, suburbs, and cities provide man-made habitats much like the natural habitats of these birds and provide abundant food sources. These birds compete aggressively for nesting sites and are ready to exploit novel nest sites. They are gregarious and live in close proximity to others of their species. They are not afraid of people. House sparrows favor the pipes of city street lights and will nest in stadiums and malls. Pigeons were brought as domesticated animals to all areas that Europeans settled. Pigeons love attics, bridges, and trestles. Because the starling is a migratory bird, it has spread from Alaska to Florida and Northern Mexico. These exotic species are now part of American wildlife.

Exotic Plants Grow Like Weeds

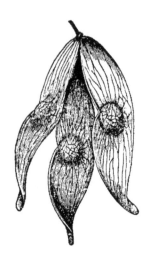

Gardeners have introduced ornamental and culinary plants and trees from Europe, Asia, and other exotic locations. Many of these introduced species have become too successful, out-competing native plants. In fields and meadows, the familiar dandelion is a perfect example of an overly successful plant. In deciduous forest areas we find the Norway maple, Sycamore maple, and Asian honeysuckle growing like weeds. The Ailantus tree or Tree of Heaven takes over disturbed areas such as vacant lots and railroad tracks. European phragmites out-competes native cattails along the shores of ponds and lakes and in other wetland areas. Many of these foreign plants do not provide useful habitat for native animals.

Exotic Insects and other Invertebrates Invade Many Ecosystems

The Asian beetle, introduced to the New York area during World War II, continues to plague gardens. More recently, waste wood has been quarantined due to the introduction of a new pest from Asia. The Asian longhorn beetle hitched a ride to New York in wooden crates or shipping palettes that were not properly aged or treated to kill the beetle larvae. The Asian longhorn beetle presents a serious threat to the trees of New York City and parts of Long Island. If not contained, it may attack the forests of the Catskills, Poconos, and Adirondacks. The beetles attack maple trees, elm, ash, horse chestnut, willow, birch, and poplar trees. The only effective means to control the beetle is to remove infested trees and destroy them by chipping or burning.

The Asian multicolored lady beetle was deliberately introduced as a biological control. This beetle is a voracious eater of garden pests such as aphids. Unfortunately, the alien lady beetle out-competes our native lady beetle species. In addition, the Asian lady beetles may winter on and in homes and other buildings.

In local coastal waters we find the exotic Asian or Japanese shore crab competing with our native crabs. The Asian shore crab was first seen on American shores in New Jersey in 1988, but now is found from Maine to North Carolina. These crabs inhabit the rocky inter-tidal zone and grow to about the size of a silver dollar. They are adaptable and omnivorous, eating algae, salt marsh grass, and small invertebrates and are able to reproduce several times a year.

Zebra mussels first appeared in the Hudson River in 1991. This species is native to the lakes of southeast Russia. It has been accidentally introduced through shipping, perhaps through the pumping out of bilge waters. It has become invasive worldwide. Zebra mussel numbers have exploded in the Hudson River. They filter the equivalent of all of the water in the estuary every 1-4 days in summer. These mussels out-compete native pearly mussels, which may be on the verge of disappearing from the river forever.

Exotic Introduced Species Are a Threat to Ecosystem Stability

Introducing exotic species into an ecosystem can result in unexpected, serious, and irreversible impacts. Highly adaptable species are more likely to become invasive than highly adapted species, but it is not always easy to predict how adaptable a species may be when exposed to new environments. Human activities create many unanticipated opportunities for introduction of exotic species into new environments.

Look out for exotic species as you explore New York City's parks and other natural areas.

Engage

NAME:

DATE:

LOCATION:

My Animal Memories

Do you have a favorite animal?

Draw a picture of your favorite animal in the environment it lives in.

Explain

My Favorite Animal Adaptations

Animals have special characteristics that help them survive in their environment. These characteristics are called *adaptations*. Adaptations can be physical or they can be behaviors.

Some adaptations may be good for both predators and prey. Running fast can help an animal catch its prey or run away from a predator. Some adaptations are only found on predators, such as sharp teeth.

Use words to describe how your favorite animal is adapted to its environment.

Explore

NAME:

DATE:

LOCATION:

My Animal Safari Field Journal Notes
Visit a zoo, park, or museum to go on safari to observe another animal carefully. Draw a picture of this animal in its environment. Try to show what it eats and what might eat it. How does it use the environment to survive? does it make?

Expand

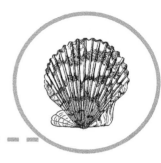
Alike and Different: Comparing Living Things

List characteristics of your favorite animal and your new animal below.

My favorite animal	My new animal

In what ways are they the same? Write those things in the overlapping space between the two circles. Write the ways they are different in the part of each circle that does not overlap.

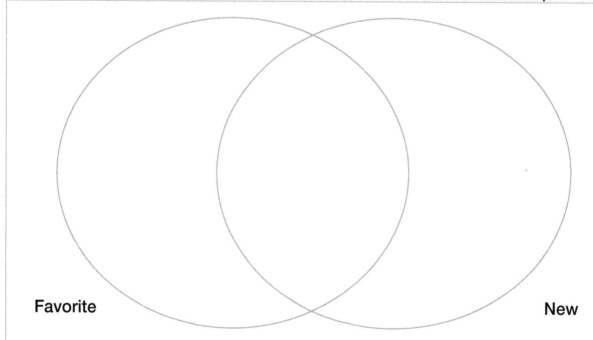

Favorite   New

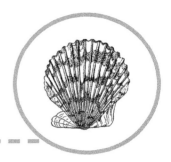

Alike and Different: Comparing Living Things

Select one animal that lives in the water and another that lives on land. List characteristics of these animals below.

Water animal	Land animal

In what ways are they the same? Write those things in the overlapping space between the two circles. Write the ways they are different in the part of each circle that does not overlap.

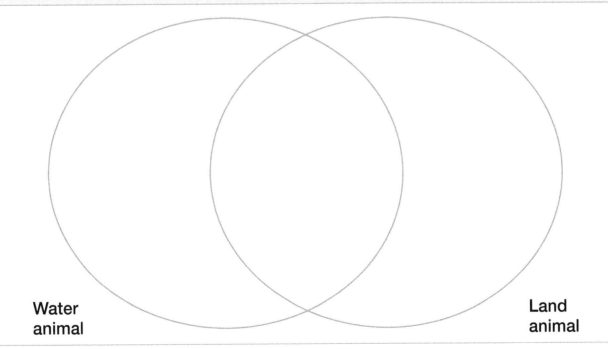

Water
animal

Land
animal

NAME:

DATE:

LOCATION:

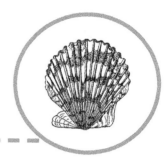

Human Impacts on Animals

How do human activities affect your favorite animal?

Use words to describe ways that humans have changed this animal's ecosystem.

Use words to describe ways that humans have hurt this animal's ecosystem.

Use words to describe ways that humans can help this animal's ecosystem.

Lakes and Ponds

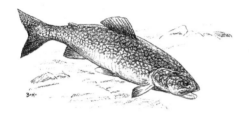

As you visit the city's parks, zoos, and botanical gardens, you will come across different bodies of water ranging from the small kettle ponds found in Alley Pond Park to the larger lakes found in Prospect Park and Flushing Meadow Park. You might observe these bodies of water and wonder what the difference is between a lake and a pond. On first glance, you might notice that size is the first difference. You are right! Although they are both standing bodies of water (they do not move like the ocean or a river or stream), ponds are often much smaller than lakes and they are also more shallow—not more than 5 or 6 feet deep. Because they are shallow, light can penetrate to the bottom of most ponds, so algae and plants can grow. Ponds often teem with life. Ponds that dry out periodically are the best habitat for breeding frogs and other amphibians, because they cannot support fish that eat the vulnerable eggs and tadpoles. In spring, these ponds ring with the calls of spring peepers and leopard frogs.

The lakes and ponds that you will find in the parks, zoos, and gardens have different origins. Some ponds were naturally formed by an underwater spring or rainwater collecting in a natural depression such as a glacial kettle. Others are human-made. Some of the lakes are also human-made, while others are naturally fed by rivers or streams. Wildlife does not care how a lake or pond was made, and both natural and artificial bodies attract birds, insects, fish, amphibians, and mammals. Lakes and ponds are great places to observe animal and plant diversity and adaptations! Although ponds are small, they are often rich in plant, insect, and bird diversity. They are great places to observe and learn about food chains and food webs in an ecosystem! While lakes are larger, you will find that they have some similar animal and plant inhabitants. Below are categories of some of the types of living things that you may encounter in and around these bodies of water.

Water-loving Plants

Plants are important to lakes and ponds because they provide food, shelter, and oxygen for other living things. Around the banks you may find tall plants such as the cattail (a member of the genus *Typha*) or the invasive phragmites, also known as the common reed. Both of these plants play a key role in filtering water. Red-winged blackbirds like to live in this habitat. Listen, you might hear one! You may also find some true aquatic plants living in the water. The duckweed you see floating on the top of the water are actually the leaves of tiny plants with small roots that dangle in the water. Because ponds are shallower, you may find a greater number and diversity of aquatic plants. Large plants like the water lily have roots buried in the sediment at the bottom of ponds. These floating plants provide food and shelter for tadpoles, frogs, turtles, and other water-living animals. There are also many microscopic plants and chlorophyll–producing organisms. Some of the parks have learning centers with microscopes that allow you to get a closer look at these organisms. You can also collect some pond or lake water to bring home or to your classroom to observe the microorganisms.

Animal Encounters

Numerous animals rely on lakes and ponds for food, shelter, and mating. In our city's ponds you may find tadpoles, frogs, salamanders, and turtles. For example, you might come across a native painted turtle. It looks very similar to the exotic introduced red-eared slider, but has a deeper shell. The first red-eared sliders in our area were probably somebody's pets, which were likely released into ponds and subsequently multiplied. This has had negative consequences for the native painted turtles, because the red-eared sliders compete with them for the same habitat and food. As a result, the native turtle population has been reduced. Red-eared sliders are native to the Carolinas, and have begun to breed in local ponds as the climate has warmed in recent years.

Lakes and ponds are great places to observe insects. You will see insects that can walk on the water! What physical adaptations allow them to do this? You will notice many different dragonflies and damselflies around a pond or lake because they lay their eggs in or near the water, often on floating vegetation. The

Science Safaris in New York City

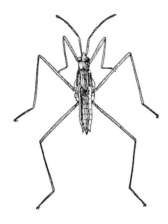

young dragonfly nymphs are aquatic and prey on mosquito larvae and other small aquatic creatures. Many other insects lay their eggs in the water, so it is a great place to find insect larvae such as mosquito larvae and mayfly larvae in the spring and summer.

Ducks, geese, and other waterfowl like to visit ponds for feeding and nesting. During the summer, you may spot a graceful white egret or a stealthy blue-grey night heron trying to capture its next fish meal. Bring a bird guide to help you identify the numerous birds you will encounter.

While you may not see many mammals during the day, several nocturnal mammals frequent the city's lakes and ponds, such as raccoons and muskrats. If you look carefully in the mud, you may find some tracks that they left behind—try to guess who was there and what they were doing. This will give you clues about the food webs and chains around the lake.

Many of our city's parks have lakes and/or ponds to explore. Some parks even offer paddleboats or canoes that allow you to have a first-hand look at the flora and fauna in and around the body of water. When you plan to visit a park, check out its website to see if there are any upcoming events that will allow you to learn more about the lake or pond habitat.

○ **Engage**

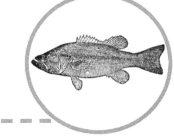

My Pond or Lake Ecosystem Drawing

Have you ever visited a pond or lake? Try to remember what you found there. Use words and/or pictures to show what you expect to find at a pond or lake.

Explore

NAME:

DATE:

LOCATION:

My Pond or Lake Ecosystem Drawing

Visit a pond or lake. Observe it carefully.
Use pictures to show what you found at the pond or lake.

Note: Return any living things to the place where you found them. If you are exploring in a National Park, you should return all objects so that others can also appreciate them.

Explain

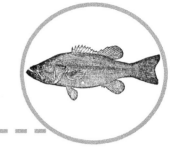

NAME:

DATE:

LOCATION:

My Pond or Lake Ecosystem Field Journal Notes

Visit a pond or lake. Observe it carefully.
Use words to describe what you found at the pond or lake.
How do these things interact?

Note: Return any living things to the place where you found them. If you are exploring in a National Park, you should return all objects so that others can also appreciate them.

Expand

Alike and Different: Comparing Living and Nonliving Things

Explore the pond or lake and collect any interesting objects you find.
Sort them into living things and nonliving things.
Draw and describe them below.

Living things	Nonliving things

Evaluate

Pond or Lake Ecosystem Human Impacts

Visit a pond or lake. Observe it carefully.

Use words to describe ways that humans have changed this pond or lake ecosystem.

Use words to describe ways that humans have hurt this pond or lake ecosystem.

Use words to describe ways that humans can help this pond or lake ecosystem.

Beaches

What is a beach? A beach is any landform along the shore of a body of water, such as a lake, an ocean, or a sea. It may consist of rocky particles, such as sand, gravel, pebbles, or cobbles. Sometimes beaches are composed of fragments of shell or coral. New York–area south shore beaches are largely composed of glacial outwash sand from the Wisconsin glacier. North shore beaches contain more pebbles and cobbles from the terminal moraine. Many local sandy beaches have black sands composed of tiny crystals of magnetite. Magnetite sand can be separated from white quartz sand with a magnet.

Beach sand, whether glacial or carried by rivers and streams to the sea, is formed by the erosion of distant mountains. Atlantic beaches are composed primarily of two minerals, quartz and feldspar, which make up the individual crystals in granite. The next time you look at a piece of polished granite, imagine the crystals eroding out of the granite to release tiny white and black or pink grains of sand.

When we think of a beach we think of sun and sand and water. These are *abiotic* factors that impact on all living things at the beach. In addition to these obvious factors, beaches are exposed to constant onshore winds and wide ranges in temperature. When you spend the day at the beach, you need sunscreen, plenty of water, and a sweater for when the sun goes down. The living things at the beach have special adaptations to help them survive in this challenging environment.

Local beaches may be exposed to the action of the Atlantic surf or may be in protected bays and backwaters. Different creatures are found in these distinctly different beach habitats.

Equilibrium and Change

We know where to find the beach, so to us it seems constant. But sand at the edge of the sea never rests in one place for very long. It is constantly moving due to the force of wind or water. Wave action and tides continuously reshape coastlines.

Other coastal geological features include barrier islands, dunes, bluffs, and upland areas. These features are formed and re-formed by the interaction between the sand and the sea. A barrier island is a sand body that lies parallel to the shore and extends above the normal high water level. Rockaway is a barrier island. It helps to protect the south shore of Brooklyn and Queens from the impact of coastal storms. Winter storms and hurricanes are important factors in the dynamic equilibrium of the shore. The mid-Atlantic coast experiences at least one major storm each year, and although hurricanes hit less often, they hit with greater fury. If you visit the beach after a storm, you will see signs of erosion. Ancient dunes may be carved back, showing layers of sand deposited when the beach was formed.

Barrier islands have unique plant communities adapted to their unique environmental conditions. Exposure to sun, extremes of temperature, wind, salt, waves, and shifting, nutrient-poor sandy soil challenges the plants that live in coastal environments. The most important abiotic factors that create these distinct habitats are exposure to tides, protection from on-shore winds resulting in sand stabilization, and soil moisture.

The beach is composed of a series of ecosystems that change with increasing distance from the ocean. Due to the effects of waves and tides, lower areas of the beach range from areas that are constantly covered by the ocean, to those that are regularly covered by the ocean, and those that are occasionally covered by the ocean such as the high tide line at full and new moons when tides are at their highest. This region is referred to as the *inter-tidal zone*.

Moving away from the inter-tidal region, you will find the upper beach and the primary dunes. These mountains of sand are exposed to harsh winds, sea spray, and the periodic attack of the ocean during storms. The primary dunes protect the secondary dunes and the valleys between known as *swales*.

Science Safaris in New York City

The swales provide protection from ocean winds and nurture plants adapted to extremes of sun, temperature, periods of intense drying, and some salt spray.

Behind the dunes, you may find marshes or maritime forests.

In the calm waters protected behind barrier islands, you will find salt marshes, the most productive of all ecosystems.

Life at the Water's Edge

When you are exploring at the beach, you will need to decide whether to explore as you walk toward the beach or away from it. There is no right or wrong, but you must choose. For this description, we will begin at the water's edge. If you are on the surf side, notice that there is nothing growing from the sand along the water's edge. This region is too harsh for plants to survive. On the bay or marsh side, you may see cordgrass growing.

Look into the water's edge and you may see silversides and striped killifish swimming in schools. These small fish are preyed upon by larger fish and birds. You may see these small fish jump to avoid young "snapper" bluefish that feed voraciously on them. But life in the ocean is most often revealed by the remains of organisms cast upon the beach. You may see dead sea skates, relatives of the shark, washed up on the shore. These eerie creatures are primitive vertebrates with a skeleton composed of cartilage rather than bone. More likely you will see their egg cases cast upon the sand at the high tide line. The egg cases are hollow black rectangles commonly called *mermaid's purses*. The tendrils at each corner were once attached to seaweed or to hard objects on the ocean bottom to keep the cases from washing ashore until the developing skate inside had hatched.

You may also see sea jellies washed up on the shore. Sea jellies were recently renamed. You may know them as jellyfish, but sea jellies are not fish at all. Fish have backbones, and sea jellies are invertebrates. Unable to swim against the ocean's currents, these delicate invertebrates are at the whim of the sea. To see living sea jellies, visit the New York Aquarium.

In June you may see horse shoe crabs that migrate to the shore in huge numbers to spawn. You may find evidence of blue crabs or other crustaceans. You may find the calcium carbonate shells of scallops, moons snails, surf or razor clams or many other mollusks.

You may find bright green, tissue-thin sea lettuce and a common brown seaweed called rockweed. These seaweeds are adapted to live at the water's edge. They are able to rehydrate and recover after drying out. A holdfast, an adaptation to life in the surf, anchors rockweed to rocks. Air bladders help the rockweed float to the surface of the water so that, even during the highest tides, the sunlight can reach them.

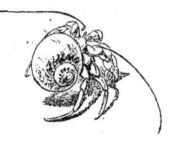

Adaptations to Moving Water and Crashing Waves

Because inter-tidal organisms essentially live both underwater and on land, they have adapted to a large range of environmental conditions. These adaptations may be behaviors, body structures, or internal functions.

Inter-tidal organisms have many adaptations to resist the motion of waves. In rocky regions at the water edge, you may find barnacles, mussels, and periwinkles. Attached to the rocks you may find small, white, cone-shaped barnacles. Barnacles remain firmly cemented in place for their whole adult life. They attach by long protein filaments called *byssal threads* and depend on the tides to

bring them water and food. Barnacles can survive even in areas of heavy, pounding surf. Like the barnacle, the blue mussel lives in a shell firmly attached to the rocks and depends on the tides for water and food. The mussel has a hinged, two-piece shell. When the water recedes, it closes its shell by means of two powerful muscles. Limpets and slipper shells have low-profile shells that allow waves and currents to flow over them. Sea stars have thousands of suctioning tube feet.

The periwinkle is a snail that feeds on the algae. It creeps along, scraping algae

from the rock surface with a rasp-like tongue. The periwinkle can attach itself firmly to rocks to withstand the pounding of the waves.

Animals that can move, such as snails and crabs, avoid high temperatures and drying by hiding in cool, moist refuges at low tide. Many prevent water loss by having waterproof outer shells, pulling completely into their shells, and sealing shut their shell opening.

Many species of birds feed on the fish and invertebrates that inhabit this zone. In summer, terns dive for silversides and killifish. Gulls are found year round.

Hills of Sand

As you walk away from the inter-tidal zone, you will see the dunes ahead. Dunes are stabilized by the plants that grow on them. Plants growing on the primary dunes must be able to withstand constant exposure to wind, salt-spray, and periodic burial by sand. In this area, only beach grass will grow. It not only survives, it thrives when buried by sand. New vertical stems sprout new leaves at the surface. The plant also spreads horizontally by rhizomes. This adaptation stabilizes the sand, resulting in the formation of dunes. The roots of this grass can reach down 40 feet to the water table beneath the dune.

A swale is the low area or valley between dunes. Plants and animals that survive in the dunes and swale have evolved several adaptations for survival in this environment. Often the plants have water-conserving adaptations. They may have thick leaves that hold water. The prickly pear cactus grows in the swales of the secondary dunes. This plant has thick, succulent leaves and a thick waxy covering that minimizes water loss from evaporation. Do not touch this plant. Its many thorns are too fine to see, but strong enough to pierce your skin. The seaside goldenrod has adapted to the upper beach by storing water in its stem. The beach pea's leaves curl up to reduce water loss through evaporation. In the swale between the primary and secondary dune, a few shrubs grow among the other beach plants, including bayberry and poison ivy. The leaves of these plants may have a waxy covering to slow evaporation. Two adaptations to bright sun include ashy or shiny leaves to reflect sunlight. Compare the leaves of plants at the beach to leaves of plants from a park. The leaves of most trees and shrubs are lighter, brighter, and thinner than those found at the beach.

Many more animals live in the dunes than on the beach. Insects, spiders, amphibians, reptiles, birds, and mammals are all represented. Ants have adapted to the harsh beach environment. Their underground tunnels protect them from the harsh summer heat. The burrowing wolf spider also burrows to escape the heat of day. It preys at night on insects. Other insects found in the dunes include wasps, grasshoppers, dragonflies, and butterflies.

Migrating birds stop in the dunes in the fall to take advantage of the berries pro-duced by bayberry, red cedar, poison ivy, greenbrier, and Virginia creeper. Most mam-mals that live in the dunes are nocturnal and their presence is revealed only by tracks and droppings. Rodents, raccoons, cottontails, and skunks are all dune inhabitants.

Protected by the secondary dunes from the direct impact of the ocean winds and salt spray, the maritime forest develops with beach plum, red cedar, wild black cherry, sumac, and pitch pine. At city beaches, white pine and Japanese black pine may have been planted to replace the native pitch pine. Several species of oak and holly are also found. The under-story of the forest is dominated by woody vines, including poison ivy and Virginia creeper.

Several species of birds, including the robin, mockingbird, thrasher, and towhee, nest in the shrub thickets and maritime forest.

Marsh Grasses

Along the sandy beaches of calm bays, a variety of marsh grasses grow. One type is the tall reed grass called phragmites, with fluffy brown tassels. You find cordgrass in the inter-tidal zone, where it is covered by water during periods of high tides. Cordgrass has adapted to survive in salty ocean water. The leaves can excrete excess salt. You may notice tiny salt crystals formed on the leaves.

Piping plovers often nest with colonies of least terns. Least terns are small relatives of gulls and nest in groups of up to a hundred pairs or more. The terns, like the plovers, lay their speckled, sand-colored eggs in a scrape in the sand. Plovers nest within the tern colonies to take advantage of their neighbor's aggressive defense of the colony. Least terns feed on the small fish that live along the water's edge. They capture prey by diving headfirst into water.

Salt Marshes

Many of our parks that hug the coast have salt marshes, usually where they are protected from the surf by the primary dunes on the bay side of the beach or by barrier islands. Salt marshes also form along the coasts of islands in the protected estuary of the Hudson River and Long Island Sound, where fresh river water and salty ocean waters mingle. Historically, many local salt marshes were filled to provide land for homes and industries because they were thought to be useless wetland areas. We have come to realize, however, that these once-perceived wastelands are actually vital ecosystems that help us in many ways. They are nurseries for fish, provide habitat and food for a host of wildlife, protect coastal areas from storms, and filter toxins from the water, protecting our bays and oceans. Although many of our original salt marshes are gone, we are lucky to have several large protected areas of marsh, including those in Jamaica Bay, Pelham Bay Park, and Marine Park. You will also find smaller salt marshes in Great Kills Park and Plum Beach.

In a typical salt marsh, you will find three distinct zones: high marsh, low marsh, and mud flat. In each of these zones, you will find characteristic animal and plant species that live there. Dotted with small dark mud snails, the mud flat is exposed only at low tide. These snails eat the algae and scavenge dead fish and shellfish that end up here. If you sieve the sand for critters, you may find clams, marine worms, and other invertebrates that lay buried in the wet sand. You may also spot a fiddler crab scurrying across the flat. These organisms provide food for fish, birds, and other animals that inhabit the marsh. The low marsh is characterized by *Spartina alterniflora*, or cordgrass. Cordgrass is a hardy plant with special glands that excrete excess salt. It has a well-anchored root system that secures it to the marsh sediment.

Lifecycle of Cordgrass

Although the cordgrasses are pretty while they are alive, it is their death and decay that provides a source of nourishment to living plants and the animals that depend on them. Bacteria and algae decompose dead marsh plants to form detritus, which then becomes the source of food for marine organisms. (The decaying leaves you find on the forest floor are also called detritus or leaf litter. They undergo a similar process as the cordgrass.) Detritus also provides nutrients for the next crop of cordgrass. The fiddler crab and ribbed mussel have developed a symbiotic relationship with the cordgrass. The animals rely on the detritus for food, the burrowing crabs aerate the roots of the plant, and the mussels' waste provides the nitrogen needed for healthy plant growth. These mollusks also filter heavy metals from the water, protecting the plants and surrounding bays and ocean from toxins. The common reed grass (*Phragmites*) grows in areas where the salt marsh has been affected by human activity. When this reed decomposes, it is not as nutritious as the cordgrass and therefore is not as useful to the marsh ecosystem.

Decaying cordgrass also forms peat. Peat is a spongy substrate that raises the level of the salt marshes, enabling different types of plants to grow. This becomes the high marsh. It is covered only during the highest tides of the month and is dominated by the taller *Spartina patens* or salt meadow cordgrass.

Insects are an important part of every ecosystem, and a salt marsh is no different. Many different types of insects live in the salt marsh. They help to aerate the roots of plants, pollinate the grasses, and are food for other insects and birds, while their larvae are food for fish and other aquatic creatures.

Jamaica Bay Wildlife Refuge

Jamaica Bay Wildlife Refuge is considered a birder's paradise because of the large numbers and diversity of waterfowl and songbirds that you can encounter there. Over the past 25 years, nearly 330 species have been sighted in the Wildlife Refuge. The refuge is especially diverse during the spring and fall migration seasons as it is an important stopover along the Atlantic Flyway, providing food and rest for many feather-winged travelers.

A good place to begin your visit to the Wildlife Refuge is the Visitor Contact Station. It is adjacent to the parking lot and houses exhibits about the wildlife, history, and current status of the bay. Rangers are available to answer questions and put you on the "right path" to explore the area. You will need a free permit to walk the trails, which you can get at the Visitor Contact Station.

West Pond

The West Pond loop trail is about 1.5 miles long and loops around a brackish, constructed pond. Along the trail you will see oaks and birch trees, bayberry and holly shrubs, marsh grasses, and native prickly pear cacti as you walk through the different ecosystems. Once you get to the pond, you can observe the variety of ducks, terns, and gulls, depending on the season. Use your bird guide to help you identify the different birds that you see. It is a fun activity to count the number of different species of birds you encounter during your visit. You will see swallows swooping to catch insects over the pond. The unusual flight patterns are easy to notice. Compare the flight of the swallows to the flight of gulls. What are the gulls hunting? What are the swallows hunting?

The refuge is also the home to a number of native reptiles and amphibians. The terrapin trail, which loops off the western part of the West Pond trail, is an important nesting site for the diamondback terrapin, a small- to medium-sized turtle that is native to the east coast. This trail is closed during nesting season. As you continue along the main trail, you will see tall nesting platforms for the osprey in the west marsh.

The trail passes through the North Garden and South Garden. These wooded areas provide food and habitat for migrating warblers and songbirds as well as some year-round residents. There are camouflaged viewing platforms that allow you to stay hidden while you observe birds around the small freshwater ponds. Raccoons, chipmunks, and other small mammals make their home here and around the refuge. Insects are also an important part of these ecosystems; for example, over 60 species of butterflies are found here.

East Pond

The East Pond trail leads you through a freshwater wetland dominated by a human-made pond. During the spring and fall migration seasons, the water level is lowered to provide mudflats for migrating shore birds. This allows them to feed on invertebrates buried in the mud. There are wooden walkways on this trail that will lead you through trees, shrubs, and tall phragmites and marsh grasses.

When you visit Jamaica Bay Wildlife Refuge, be sure to bring a hat, sunscreen, insect repellant, and sturdy shoes that are either waterproof or that you do not mind getting wet. Bring your binoculars, bird guide, and notebook so you can note the different species that you encounter. The Visitor Contact Center has a bookstore that sells nature guides and other books that provide information about the natural and cultural history of Jamaica Bay.

New York City Beaches

Most New York City beaches are heavily used for recreation and have lost much of their wildness. The following beaches offer a glimpse of the once-wild waterfront of the city.

Coney Island

Almost a century before the boardwalk opened along the Atlantic Ocean, Coney Island was on its way to becoming the nation's most popular pleasure ground. Coney Island was established as a seaside resort in 1824. The BMT subway line reached the area in 1920, making the beach accessible to the whole city. Coney Island is an enduring symbol of New York City and its most famous playground. Attendance on a hot summer day sometimes reaches a million sunbathers. Coney Island is most valuable to the student of natural science as an opportunity to compare a highly used beach with those that have experienced less human impact. Look for signs of the intensive use, including the development of buildings and the boardwalk so close to the water's edge. You may also find evidence of life in the ocean along the beach, along with litter and other evidence of human overuse. A visit to Coney Island can easily be combined with a visit to the New York Aquarium, which is located at Coney Island and is among it best-known attractions.

Dead Horse Bay

Dead Horse Bay, located in Brooklyn, across the street from Floyd Bennett Field, is a small body of water with an interesting history. The Dutch built wheat mills here during the 17th century to use the power of the tides to grid wheat into flour. You can see a remaining millstone along the Millstone trail as you approach the bay.

How did this bay get its name? Dead Horse Bay has a sordid history as the location of horse-rendering plants, garbage incinerators, and fish oil factories. Dead horses from the city's streets were turned in to glue and fertilizer, and the chopped-up bones were dumped into the local waters. Often the remains of the horses would wash up along the shores, hence the name. With the discovery of menhaden or porgy in the bay, plants were opened to process fish oil and the remains of fish and other dead animals into fertilizer. You could only imagine the sights and smells of the bay at that time! The city later turned the surrounding marshes into a landfill that was capped in the 1930s, only for the cap to burst in the 1950s, spewing decades of trash into the bay.

Today, Dead Horse Bay is a part of the Gateway National Recreation Area; however, you can see remnants of its squalid past—including horse bones and old bottles—strewn along the shore. Although evidence of human impact on the environment is strong, nature has reclaimed much of the land surrounding the bay with marsh grasses and shrubs. Red-winged blackbirds live in the grasses and egrets hunt for fish along the shores of the bay. It has become a popular place for school groups

Science Safaris in New York City

to seine for fish, sieve the sand for organisms, and learn about the cultural and natural history of the surrounding area.

Fort Tilden

Fort Tilden, now part of Gateway National Recreation Area on the Rockaway Peninsula, was kept wild as the most modern addition to the fortifications of New York Harbor. Its grounds include some of the most secluded and unspoiled beaches in New York.

Today the park's former role in harbor defense can be seen in the remaining past military structures amid the reclaimed natural areas. There are many great spots to see wildlife. The primary dunes protect an emerging successional maritime forest. Walk through the dunes at designated paths and observe the changing plants found in the dunes and the more protected swales between the dunes.

At the ocean's edge along the Atlantic shore, comb the beach for signs of the life below the tide. Use a field guide to Atlantic seashells to help you identify the different mollusks that inhabit the offshore sea. You may also find horseshoe crabs and blue crabs. Be on the watch for the invading Asian shore crabs. Watch and listen for amphibians, insects, and birds near the fort's freshwater pond. The observatory deck on top of Battery Harris East, a historic gun site, is a great spot to watch migrating birds as well as resident hawks. You may also observe the migration of Monarch butterflies in spring and fall. This spot also offers expansive views of Jamaica Bay and New York Harbor. You can see across to Sandy Hook, New Jersey at the far edge of the harbor.

Orchard Beach

Orchard Beach is located in Pelham Bay Park. This beach differs from most local beaches because it is not a sandy beach. It is a human-made beach that borders Long Island Sound. It is not exposed to the rough waves of the ocean beaches, and sand is not deposited on this beach by ocean currents as it is on most other local beaches. But Orchard Beach is exposed to rapidly changing tides and storm waves from Long Island Sound. The Hunter Island Marine Zoology and Geology Sanctuary is located on the north side of the beach. A walk to this area of the beach will reveal a number of geological features. You will encounter bedrock that has been exposed by erosion due to storm waves from Long Island Sound as well as large erratics that were dropped there by the Wisconsin glacier. Glacial till covers the bedrock—note the variety of rounded pebbles and rocks that you see along the shore. Remember that local rock is mostly Manhattan mica schist, Inwood marble, or Fordham gneiss. Do these rocks look like the local rocks? How do you think they became so smooth and rounded?

Plum Beach

Plum Beach was known as Plum Island until 1940. Robert Moses filled in the island, connecting it to Brooklyn to make way for the Belt Parkway. However, in a striking demonstration of the power of erosion, the beach is slowly reclaiming the parkway. Plumb Beach is protected from the strong ocean currents by Rockaway Barrier Island; however, the beach is not protected from the loss of sands by the currents that move from the west to east. Long shore drift at Plum Beach occurs when sand from the west is moved by the tide at an angle to the shore and deposited in the east. Since there is no sand to naturally replace the sand that is lost in the west, the shoreline becomes diminished and erosion occurs. The bike path that once hugged the beach has eroded away and the Belt Parkway is now threatened. There are different solutions currently being considered to protect the beach and parkway, including building groynes (a structure designed to disrupt water flow and reduce erosion) or relocating the bike path and parkway. Beach nourishment is the process of replacing sand on a beach. It is a possible solution for Plum Beach, but unless the flow of the water is controlled, the replaced sand would simply move to the east.

This is an important ecosystem to protect not only because of the high volume of traffic that depends upon the Belt Parkway. Plum Beach also provides vital habitat to a number of shorebirds, horseshoe crabs, and a host of other wildlife that live in the mud. On the tidal mudflats at Plum Beach, you can observe small eastern mud snails feeding on algae and scavenging dead crabs. You can dig for soft-shelled clams and other animals that live in the mud. The salt marshes and tidal lagoon provide habitat for shorebirds and mollusks. It is also a great place for exploring the sand dunes. Note the kinds of plants you see growing here; these help hold the dunes together. Do not walk on the dunes, however; these are fragile ecosystems, and human feet could damage them. Follow the edge of the shore and compare the ocean side of the flats to the more protected inlet. Notice how the dunes help to protect the inner shore.

Every year around the full moon in May, you can observe the horseshoe crabs mating. These amazing ancient animals have remained unchanged for over 200 million years. The male, much smaller that the female, uses its mitten-looking claws to hang on to the female as she crawls up the beach during the high tide to lay her eggs. As she digs holes and lays a couple of thousand eggs at a time, the male fertilizes them, then she covers the holes with sand. The eggs will take up to two weeks to hatch. These eggs are a vital source of food for migrating shorebirds. A quick web search will find several groups offering walks during horseshoe crab mating season.

Engage

My Beach Ecosystem Memories

Have you ever visited a beach? Try to remember what you found there.

Use words and/or pictures to show what you expect to find at a beach.

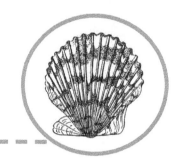

My Beach Ecosystem Drawing

Visit a beach. Observe it carefully.
Use pictures to show what you found at the beach.

Note: Return any living things to the place where you found them. If you are exploring on a National seashore, you should return all objects so that others can also appreciate them.

Explain

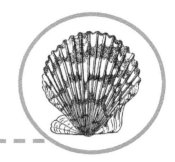

My Beach Ecosystem Field Journal Notes
Visit a beach. Observe it carefully. Use words to describe what you found at the beach. How do these things interact?

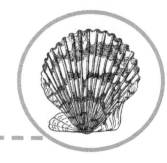

Alike and Different: Comparing Living and Nonliving Things

Explore the beach and collect any interesting objects you find.
Draw and describe them below.

Living things	Nonliving things

Evaluate

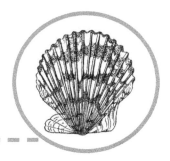

NAME:

DATE:

LOCATION:

Beach Ecosystem Human Impacts
Visit a beach. Observe it carefully.

Use words to describe ways that humans have changed this beach ecosystem.

Use words to describe ways that humans have hurt this beach ecosystem.

Use words to describe ways that humans can help this beach ecosystem. |
| |

NAME:

DATE:

LOCATION:

My Saltmarsh/Estuary Ecosystem Drawing

Have you ever visited a saltmarsh? Draw a picture of a saltmarsh that you have visited before. Try to remember what you found there. Use words and/or pictures to show what you expect to find at a saltmarsh/estuary.

NAME:

DATE:

LOCATION:

My Saltmarsh/Estuary Ecosystem Drawing

Visit a saltmarsh. Observe it carefully.
Use words and/or pictures to show what you found at the saltmarsh.

Note: Return any living things to the place where you found them. If you are exploring on a National seashore, you should return all objects so that others can also appreciate them.

Alike and Different: Comparing Living and Nonliving Things

Explore the saltmarsh/estuary and collect any interesting objects you find.
Draw and describe them below.

Living things	Nonliving things

Appendix

New York City Elementary and Middle School Science Scope and Sequence Chart

Kindergarten

Unit 1 Trees through the Season	Unit 2 How Do We Observe and Describe Objects?	Unit 3 Animals
• Botanical gardens • Parks	• New York Hall of Science • Various sites	• Brooklyn Children's Museum • Zoos • Parks • Queens County Farm Museum • American Museum of Natural History

Grade 1

Unit 1 Animal Diversity	Unit 2 Properties of Matter	Unit 3 Changes Between Seasons
• Brooklyn Children's Museum • Zoos • Parks • Salt marshes • Beaches	• New York Hall of Science • Brooklyn Children's Museum	• New York Hall of Science • Botanical gardens • Central Park Weather Station

Grade 2

Unit 1 Earth Materials	Unit 2 Forces and Motion	Unit 3 Plant Diversity
• American Museum of Natural History • Parks • Beaches	• New York Hall of Science • Beaches	• Botanical gardens • Parks • Salt marshes

(continues)

New York City Elementary and Middle School Science
Scope and Sequence Chart (continued)

Grade 3

Unit 1 Matter	Unit 2 Energy	Unit 3 Simple Machines	Unit 4 Plant and Animal Adaptations
• New York Hall of Science	• New York Hall of Science • QBG Green Building	• New York Hall of Science • Brooklyn Children's Museum	• Zoos • Botanical gardens • American Museum of Natural History

Grade 4

Unit 1 Animals and Plants in Their Environment	Unit 2 Electricity and Magnetism	Unit 3 Properties of Water	Unit 4 Interactions of Air, Water, and Land
• Zoos • Botanical gardens • American Museum of Natural History • Parks	• New York Hall of Science	• Brooklyn Children's Museum	• American Museum of Natural History • Beaches and parks

Grade 5

Unit 1 Nature of Science	Unit 2 Earth Science	Unit 3 Food and Nutrition	Unit 4 Exploring Ecosystems
• All sites	• AMNH (HoPE) • Beaches and parks	• Brooklyn Children's Museum • New York Hall of Science	• Botanical gardens • Zoos • Brooklyn Children's Museum • AMNH • Parks, salt marshes, and beaches

Grade 6

Unit 1 Simple and Complex Machines	Unit 2 Weather	Unit 3 Diversity of Life	Unit 4 Interdependence
• New York Hall of Science	• Beaches • Central Park Weather Station	• Zoos • Botanical gardens • Parks, salt marshes, and beaches • American Museum of Natural History • Brooklyn Children's Museum	• Salt marshes • Parks • American Museum of Natural History • Brooklyn Children's Museum

Grade 7

Unit 1 Geology	Unit 2 Interactions Between Matter and Energy	Unit 3 Dynamic Equilibrium: The Human Animal	Unit 4 Dynamic Equilibrium: Other Organisms
• American Museum of Natural History • Parks and beaches	• New York Hall of Science • Beaches		• Zoos • Botanical gardens

Grade 8

Unit 1 Reproduction, Heredity, and Evolution	Unit 2 Forces and Motion on Earth	Unit 3 Earth, Sun, Moon System	Unit 4 Humans in their Environment: Needs and Tradeoffs
• American Museum of Natural History • Zoos • Botanical gardens • Queens County Farm Museum	• New York Hall of Science	• American Museum of Natural History • New York Hall of Science	• Queens Botanical Garden's Green Building • Salt marshes • Zoos • Queens County Farm Museum